AI Development for the Modern World: Shaping the Future with Intelligent Systems

A Comprehensive Guide to Building and Integrating AI Solutions

Samantha Reed

Table of Contents

INTRODUCTION

Artificial intelligence (AI) is at the front of a technological revolution occurring at a speed never seen before. AI is changing industries, reinventing our daily lives, and rewriting the future in various fields, including healthcare, finance, entertainment, and transportation. Designed to be your go-to resource for comprehending and utilizing AI, "AI Development for the Modern World: Shaping the Future with Intelligent Systems: A Comprehensive Guide to Building and Integrating AI Solutions."

From foundational concepts to advanced applications, this book offers a thorough exploration of artificial intelligence. It delivers valuable insights into the development and deployment of AI solutions, bridging the gap between theory and real-world application. Whether you're a novice seeking to grasp the basics or a seasoned professional aiming to broaden your expertise, this guide is tailored to your needs.

Our journey through this book will delve into essential AI topics such as computer vision, natural language processing, deep learning, and machine learning. You'll learn how to collect and preprocess data, build and refine models, and apply AI to practical challenges. To prepare you for the dynamic nature of this field, we'll also discuss the ethical considerations and future directions of AI.

Join us as we explore AI's possibilities and use intelligent systems to reshape the future.

CHAPTER I

Understanding Artificial Intelligence

Definition and history of AI

Artificial intelligence, or AI, is the simulation of human intelligence in computers created to think and learn like humans. These artificial intelligence systems can carry out speech recognition, visual perception, decision-making, and language translation, which generally need human intelligence. AI's main objective is to build computers that can carry out complicated activities independently, complementing human abilities and increasing productivity in various industries.

The idea of artificial intelligence (AI) dates back to ancient times when many societies were familiar with myths and tales of artificial entities endowed with intelligence. However, the middle of the 20th century saw the formal establishment of AI as a scientific field. John McCarthy first used the phrase "Artificial Intelligence" in 1956 at the Dartmouth Conference, which is seen as the beginning of AI research.

Beginning in the 1950s and lasting until the 1970s, AI research was characterized by great optimism and lofty objectives. Researchers created early artificial intelligence (AI) algorithms to solve mathematical puzzles, play chess games, and demonstrate logical truths. These early achievements raised optimistic views regarding AI's future. But this time, sometimes called the "golden era" of artificial intelligence, was quickly succeeded by a depressing period called the "AI winter." The unmet expectations and technological constraints of the available AI methodologies caused progress to stop and funding for AI research to decline during the AI winter of the 1970s and 1980s.

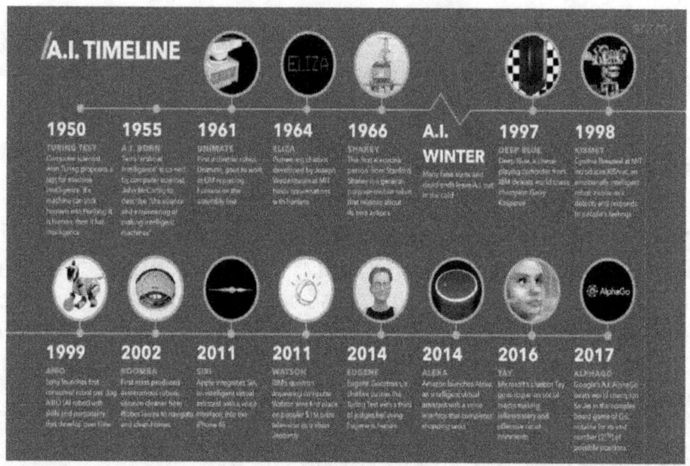

The shortcomings of symbolic AI, which mainly depended on logic and rule-based systems, were exposed during the AI winter. Tasks requiring common sense reasoning, comprehension of natural language, and experience-based learning were complex for these systems. Consequently, scientists started looking into different strategies, which brought about the development of machine learning in the 1980s. As a branch of artificial intelligence, machine learning focuses on creating algorithms that let computers learn from data and get better over time without needing to be explicitly programmed.

There are various reasons for the comeback of AI in the late 1990s and early 2000s. First, the infrastructure required to support complex AI models was made possible by the exponential expansion in computational capacity brought about by hardware breakthroughs and the introduction of GPUs. The internet's spread produced second, massive volumes of data and the digital revolution, and these data sources fed machine learning algorithms. Finally, advances in machine learning methods, especially the creation of deep learning and neural networks, completely changed the field of AI study.

Utilizing artificial neural networks with numerous layers—hence the term "deep"—deep learning is a subset of machine learning that models intricate patterns in data. Some historic successes in the 2010s exemplified deep learning's success. ImageNet is a benchmark for picture identification, and in 2012, a deep learning model created by academics at the University of Toronto won the competition by a wide margin. This triumph raised awareness of deep learning and encouraged investment in the field.

After this discovery, artificial intelligence systems started functioning at superhuman levels across various fields. For example, in 2016, Google's DeepMind created AlphaGo, an artificial intelligence software that beat the world champion Go player—a feat initially predicted to take decades to achieve. Similarly, artificial intelligence (AI) systems have advanced significantly in natural language processing, as demonstrated by creating models like OpenAI's GPT-3, which can produce writing that resembles a person's and execute various language tasks with great skill.

Despite its remarkable progress, artificial intelligence still grapples with numerous challenges and ethical dilemmas. Addressing issues such as bias in AI algorithms, privacy concerns, and potential job displacement requires careful consideration and responsible governance. As technology continues to advance, it is crucial to ensure that AI systems are fair, transparent, and aligned with human values.

The development of AI is a testament to human perseverance and ingenuity. Thanks to the collective efforts of academics, engineers, and visionaries, artificial intelligence (AI) has evolved from its humble beginnings to the sophisticated systems of today. Looking ahead, AI holds the potential to address some of the most pressing challenges facing humanity and unlock unprecedented opportunities.

Types of AI: Narrow AI, General AI, and Superintelligent AI

Three main categories can be used to categorize artificial intelligence (AI): narrow AI, general AI, and superintelligent AI. These divisions aid in assessing the present state of AI systems and forecasting their future development. A different level of machine intelligence is represented by each form of AI, which varies in complexity, capacity, and possible social influence.

The most common type of AI is narrow AI, sometimes called weak AI. It is made to carry out a single task or a small number of activities very well. Narrow artificial intelligence (AI) systems are highly specialized and proficient in specific domains, including autonomous vehicles, recommendation systems, picture recognition, and language translation. These systems are constrained by the extent of their programming and training data and function according to a predetermined set of rules. For instance, a voice assistant like Alexa or Siri can comprehend and react to voice instructions. Still, it cannot carry out activities that are not part of its programming or comprehend context that is not part of its training. The principal benefit of Narrow AI is its capacity to mechanize monotonous jobs, optimize productivity, and yield insights that people would need more annually.

Artificial General Intelligence (AGI), or Strong AI or General AI, is a higher degree of machine intelligence that is still mostly theoretical. General artificial intelligence aims to build machines that can learn, comprehend, and apply knowledge to various tasks, much like humans. In contrast to Narrow AI, which is exceptional in particular fields, General AI can carry out any intellectual work that a person can. It would be capable of reasoning, planning, problem-solving, abstract thought, understanding complicated concepts, experience-based learning, and situational adaptation. Significant progress in our knowledge of the human brain and in simulating its functions in machines would be necessary to achieve general artificial intelligence. Contextual comprehension, emotional intelligence, and common sense reasoning are all essential for developing AGI, which presents significant technical obstacles. While many experts think that artificial intelligence (AI) has the potential to transform numerous industries and bring forth previously unheard-of scientific breakthroughs, it also poses severe ethical and societal issues.

Artificial Superintelligence (ASI), often known as superintelligent AI, is the fictitious future condition in which AI outperforms human intelligence in every discipline. In addition to surpassing humans at certain activities, superintelligent AI would be cognitively superior in domains like creativity, problem-solving, and emotional intelligence. With this degree of intelligence, ASI can carry out currently incomprehensible jobs for humans, which would result in quick advances in science, technology, and other areas. Thinkers like Nick Bostrom popularized Superintelligent AI by highlighting the advantages and disadvantages of developing such sophisticated systems. On the one hand, artificial intelligence (ASI) has the potential to address and even eradicate poverty and some of the world's most serious problems, like sickness. However, existential threats may arise if ASI progress needs to be appropriately regulated.

A foundation for comprehending the development of AI technology and its possible ramifications is provided by the differences between Narrow AI, General AI, and Superintelligent AI. With its specific powers, narrow AI is already revolutionizing sectors and raising productivity levels in people. While theoretical, general artificial intelligence (AI) symbolizes the goal of building machines that can think like humans. It provides both tremendous hurdles and great potential for progress.

The evolution of AI will influence technology and society in the future as it moves from narrow AI to general AI and possibly even superintelligent AI. To fully utilize AI, it will be necessary to seize the chances while resolving the difficulties and moral dilemmas. To guarantee that these technologies are created and applied in ways that benefit humanity, cooperation between researchers, legislators, and society is necessary for increasingly sophisticated AI systems.

Key concepts: Machine Learning, Deep Learning, Neural Networks

Machine learning, a pivotal branch of artificial intelligence, lays the foundation for the discipline's development. It enables computers to learn from data, improve over time, and make predictions or decisions. This transformative technology has significantly influenced how machines perceive and interact with their environment, particularly in processing data, identifying patterns, and making judgments.

A branch of artificial intelligence called machine learning (ML) focuses on creating algorithms that let computers analyze, interpret, and forecast data to make judgments or predictions. In contrast to traditional programming, which requires humans to code explicit instructions, machine learning entails training a model on a sizable dataset. The model may make predictions on fresh, unknown data by using the patterns and relationships it has learned from the data throughout the training process. The fundamental characteristic of machine learning is its capacity to learn from experience, which makes it an extremely effective tool for tasks like image identification, natural language processing, and predictive analytics. The three primary categories of machine learning are reinforcement, unsupervised, and supervised learning. A labeled dataset is used to train the model in supervised learning, where each training example has an output label associated with it.

Artificial neural networks are used in deep learning, a specific area of machine learning, to model and resolve complicated issues. These networks are described as "deep" because they employ numerous layers, enabling them to learn and represent data at different levels of abstraction. Deep learning is becoming increasingly popular since it works well with massive amounts of data and beats conventional machine learning algorithms for many jobs. Deep learning models, sometimes called deep neural networks, are designed with layers of interconnected "neurons" that process information, emulating the structure of the human brain. These models' ability to extract features from unprocessed data autonomously removes the need for human feature engineering. This capacity makes deep learning particularly useful in disciplines like computer vision, where it can distinguish and categorize objects in images, and natural language processing, where it can interpret and synthesize human language. Two common varieties of deep learning architectures are Convolutional Neural Networks (CNNs) and Recurrent Neural Networks (RNNs).

Neural networks are the fundamental idea behind both deep learning and machine learning. A neural network is a computing model created to mimic the information-processing capabilities of biological neural networks found in the human brain. These networks comprise layers of networked nodes or neurons that can each be calculated straightforwardly. Neural networks' capacity for learning and adaptation through training gives them power. Based on the mistakes in its predictions, the network modifies the weights of the connections between neurons during training. Backpropagation is spreading the error throughout the network in a backward direction while adjusting the weights to reduce the error.

Significant advances in AI have been made due to the interaction between deep learning, neural networks, and machine learning. The basis is provided by machine learning, which allows machines to learn from data and improve over time. Deep learning expands on this foundation by using neural networks to handle increasingly complicated and high-dimensional data. The computer framework that enables these learning processes is provided by neural networks, whose architecture is inspired by the brain's structure. When taken as a whole, these ideas have sparked innovations in fields, including autonomous systems, natural language comprehension, and image and speech recognition. Deep learning algorithms, for example, have been used to create self-driving cars that can maneuver through challenging environments, medical diagnostic tools that can accurately identify diseases from medical images, and language translation services that can translate text fluently between multiple languages.

While these technologies hold immense potential, they also present significant challenges. For instance, training deep learning models is resource-intensive and requires vast amounts of data and computational power. Moreover, these models often operate as 'black boxes,' making it difficult to understand their decision-making process. This raises important questions about accountability and transparency.

In summary, machine learning, deep learning, and neural networks are the cornerstones of modern AI. Machine learning provides the ability to learn from data, deep learning enhances this capability with powerful neural network topologies, and neural networks provide the computational structure. Together, they have transformed AI from a theoretical concept into a practical technology with a wide range of applications, driving innovation and shaping the future of numerous industries.

Ethical considerations in AI development

The ethical implications of artificial intelligence (AI) have become increasingly important as it develops and becomes more integrated into all facets of society. To guarantee that AI systems are advantageous, equitable, and consistent with human values, several ethical concerns are brought up by the development and application of AI technology. The development of AI must consider several critical ethical factors, such as prejudice and justice, accountability and transparency, privacy, the effect on employment, and the wider societal consequences of AI.

Among the most important ethical problems in AI are bias and fairness. Since AI systems are taught on big datasets, they are likely to reinforce and even magnify biases found in these datasets. In several applications, including loan approval systems, recruiting algorithms, and law enforcement tools, this may result in unfair and discriminatory consequences. For instance, an AI system trained on past hiring data would come to prioritize some demographics over others, maintaining current disparities. Careful analysis of the training data, the algorithms employed, and the deployment scenario are necessary to ensure fairness in AI. Researchers and developers must employ algorithmic openness, diversified data sourcing, and bias detection to discover and reduce biases.

Accountability and transparency are also essential ethical factors. AI systems frequently function as "black boxes," meaning humans have difficulty understanding how they make decisions. This lack of openness can result in a lack of confidence and responsibility, particularly when AI systems are applied in crucial fields like banking, criminal justice, and healthcare. Developers and legislators support explainable AI as a solution to this problem, which entails creating AI systems whose functions are simple to comprehend and interpret. Explainable AI makes it possible for judgments made by AI systems to be carefully considered and rationalized, which fosters responsibility and confidence. Establishing distinct lines of accountability is also necessary to determine who bears responsibility for mistakes or harm caused by AI systems.

Another primary ethical concern in AI development is privacy. For AI systems to work well, much personal data is frequently required. Sensitive information about people's identities, preferences, and activities may be included in this data. Data protection and privacy are issues brought up by gathering, storing, and analyzing such data. Robust data protection techniques, including anonymization, encryption, and safe data storage, must be implemented to guarantee that AI systems respect user privacy. Developers need also abide by privacy rules and regulations, such as the European Union's General Data Protection Regulation (GDPR), which establishes stringent guidelines for data processing procedures. Users should have control over their data and be informed about its use.

One crucial ethical concern that has received much attention is how AI will affect jobs. Artificial Intelligence (AI) carries the risk of job displacement, even if technology might increase efficiency and open up new career prospects. This is especially true for repetitive and routine occupations. AI-driven automation can improve social unrest and economic inequality by eliminating jobs across various industries. Proactive steps are needed to address the job impact of AI, such as reskilling and upskilling programs to assist workers in adjusting to new roles that call for human ingenuity and talent. Together, industry leaders and policymakers must devise plans that balance social welfare and scientific growth to guarantee that artificial intelligence's advantages are shared relatively throughout society.

The development of AI also poses more enormous societal ramifications, which go beyond these immediate ethical issues. It is necessary to recognize how AI may affect and mold social norms, behaviors, and power relations. For example, AI systems employed in social media platforms can influence political dialogue and public opinion by selecting and promoting particular material. This questions how AI fits into information integrity, freedom of speech, and democracy. Human dignity, rights, and welfare must be given priority when developing ethical rules and principles to ensure that AI systems are employed in ways that advance societal good. Developing AI policy that reflects a range of viewpoints and values requires multi-stakeholder interaction, including feedback from ethicists, social scientists, and the general public.

Furthermore, worldwide cooperation and harmonization of ethical standards are important due to the global character of AI research. It's reassuring to know that developing a unified and uniform framework, despite its challenges due to differing ethical standards and legal frameworks across different nations, is possible. In order to promote discussion and cooperation on AI ethics, international organizations like the United Nations and the Organization for Economic Cooperation and Development (OECD) are essential. Global norms and guidelines can be established to assist in guaranteeing that AI technologies are created and applied in a manner that is compliant with fundamental human rights and values.

In conclusion, there are many different and intricate ethical factors to take into mind when developing AI.

These factors include prejudice and justice, accountability and transparency, privacy, employment, and wider social effects. It's crucial to involve academics, developers, politicians, and society at large in a comprehensive and cooperative strategy to address these ethical concerns. By putting ethical principles and human-centered values first, we can utilize AI to improve human well-being while reducing risks and making sure that the advantages are distributed fairly. To ensure that artificial intelligence (AI) is used responsibly in the future and contributes positively to society, responsible AI development and use are crucial.

CHAPTER II

Foundations of AI Development

Introduction to algorithms and data structures

The fundamental building blocks of computer science, algorithms, and data structures are necessary for effective problem-solving and program development. Anyone working in programming has to grasp these ideas because they offer the processes and instruments required to handle data and carry out intricate tasks efficiently.

An algorithm is a systematic process or a collection of guidelines that must be followed when performing calculations or other problem-solving tasks, particularly by a computer. It is a detailed set of instructions that outlines how to carry out a specific action or address a particular issue. The ability of computers to process data and carry out operations that would be impractical or impossible for humans to carry out manually makes algorithms essential. They span from easy tasks like adding two integers to difficult ones like organizing massive datasets or figuring out which path in a network is the shortest.

On the other hand, data structures are methods for effectively accessing and modifying data by arranging and storing it in a computer. They specify how the actions that can be carried out on the data relate. Arrays, linked lists, stacks, queues, trees, and graphs are common data structures. Every data structure suits a distinct set of applications and has pros and cons. Selecting the appropriate data structure is essential since it directly affects an algorithm's effectiveness and performance.

The way algorithms and data structures work well together is evidence of their synergy. It can operate effectively only when a suitable data structure backs a well-designed algorithm. Take the task of looking for a particular object in a data collection. The procedure would have to inspect each element individually if the data were stored in an unsorted array, requiring a linear search with an $O(n)$ time complexity. However, because of the characteristics of the tree structure, the same search operation can be carried out significantly more quickly with a time complexity of $O(\log n)$ if the data is stored in a binary search tree.

The array is one of the basic data structures. A group of elements with corresponding keys or indexes is called an array. It offers a straightforward method for accessing and storing a set number of elements in a single, continuous memory block. Arrays are commonly utilized because of their ease of use and $O(1)$ constant-time access to elements. They may be limited by their fixed size, though, and adding or removing pieces may need to be more efficient if it necessitates moving other aspects.

Linked lists solve a few of arrays' drawbacks. Every node in a linked list has a data element and a reference, or link, to the node after it in the list's sequence. This structure makes it possible to insert and remove elements quickly and efficiently and to resize them dynamically by simply altering the nodes' references. However, because linked lists store references, they have a more significant memory overhead and a time complexity of $O(n)$ for searching, which makes it slower to access entries.

Specialized data structures called stacks and queues function according to the ideas of "last in, first out" (LIFO) and "first in, first out" (FIFO), respectively. A stack is helpful when retrieving the most current element first is necessary since it permits the addition and deletion of elements from its top end. In contrast, a queue can be used for activities where elements must be processed in the order they were added because it permits insertion at one end (the rear) and deletion at the other (the front).

Trees are data structures with a hierarchical structure comprising nodes connected by edges. Every node can have offspring nodes, forming a parent-child relationship. The highest node is referred to as the root. Binary trees are especially significant since each node can have a maximum of two children. Binary search trees (BSTs) are a particular kind of binary tree in which the value of the left child node is less than the value of the parent, and the value of the right child node is more excellent. With an average time, complexity of O(log n), this feature makes efficient searching, insertion, and deletion operations possible.

Graphs are more intricate structures of connected nodes (vertices) called edges. They can be used to symbolize a variety of issues, such as transportation systems and social networks. These structures are traversed and explored using graph algorithms like depth-first search (DFS) and breadth-first search (BFS). The shortest path between nodes is determined using more complex methods, such as the A* and Dijkstra's algorithms, and is essential for applications like GPS navigation.

Big O notation, which expresses the upper bound of the algorithm's execution time or space requirements regarding the input size, is frequently used to gauge an algorithm's efficiency. For instance, if the input size doubles, an algorithm with an O(n^2) time complexity will take around four times longer to execute. This notation makes it easier to evaluate the effectiveness of many algorithms and choose the best one for a specific task.

To sum up, the core ideas of computer science that facilitate effective data processing and problem-solving are algorithms and data structures. Tasks are carried out step-by-step by algorithms, and data structures specify how the data is organized. Selecting the appropriate data format and algorithm is essential for maximizing effectiveness and efficiency. When programmers grasp these ideas, they may create and use solutions that efficiently manage complicated issues and big datasets. Algorithms and data structures are essential for building reliable, effective, scalable software solutions, even as technology develops.

Basics of programming languages used in AI (Python, R, etc.)

The foundation of current artificial intelligence development is the fundamentals of programming languages used in AI, such as Python, R, and others. These languages are appropriate for various AI applications, including robotics, natural language processing, data analysis, and machine learning. They also include a variety of features and tools. Comprehending the fundamentals of these programming languages is crucial for anyone wishing to pursue a career in artificial intelligence.

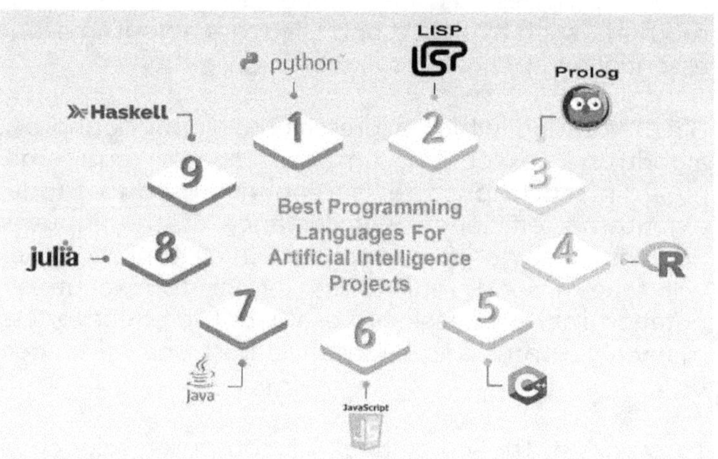

The most widely used programming language in the AI space is Python. Because of its readability and simplicity, it's an excellent option for novice and seasoned coders. The many libraries and frameworks available for Python, including Scikit-learn, TensorFlow, Keras, and PyTorch, offer reliable resources for creating and implementing AI models. Google's TensorFlow is especially well-suited for deep learning and large-scale machine learning applications. Compared to TensorFlow, PyTorch is more versatile and more straightforward to debug since it provides a dynamic computational graph built by Facebook's AI Research division. The creation of neural networks is made more accessible with Keras, an interface for the TensorFlow library that makes neural network creation more approachable for people without much programming knowledge.

Furthermore, Python is more versatile than AI-specific libraries. Because of its general-purpose nature, developers can use the same language to handle deployment, visualization, and even preparation of data. Libraries like NumPy and Pandas are crucial for data manipulation and numerical computations. Matplotlib and Seaborn are frequently used to create visuals that help comprehend data trends and model performance. Python is a one-stop shop for many AI practitioners due to its seamless integration with other languages and tools, further increasing its usefulness in AI projects.

R is another strong language frequently used in AI, primarily for statistical analysis and data visualization. R's strength is how easily it can handle complex data processing and how thorough its statistical capabilities are. Because of its vast package ecology, it is highly preferred in academics and research. For machine learning tasks, libraries like caret, random Forest, and XGBoost are frequently utilized, and ggplot2 is well known for its sophisticated data visualization features. Despite being distinct from Python, R's syntax is quite expressive for statistical operations, which can significantly help when working on complex data analysis jobs.

R is also very good at managing big datasets and offers many choices for manipulating data using packages like data. Table and dplyr. Because of its ability to be integrated with other data processing tools like Hadoop and Spark, R is a compelling language for big data applications. Furthermore, interactive web apps may be made with R's Shiny package. This feature lets users create and share interactive dashboards and data visualizations, which help share AI model insights.

Although R and Python are AI's most widely used languages, a few other languages are also essential to note. For example, Java is renowned for its speed and scalability, which makes it appropriate for production settings and large-scale AI systems. Its relevance in AI is further cemented by its usage in large data frameworks such as Hadoop and Apache Spark. Java is a dependable alternative for creating sophisticated artificial intelligence systems due to its extensive use in enterprise settings and object-oriented solid characteristics.

Another language that's essential to performance-intensive applications is C++, despite being less popular for advanced AI development. Because of its speed and efficiency, it is perfect for creating AI algorithms that need much processing power, such as real-time image processing and game creation. C++ is utilized to develop deep learning and neural network acceleration libraries such as TensorRT and Caffe to take advantage of its performance benefits.

In the AI world, Julia is a new language well-known for its user-friendliness and excellent performance. Combining the simplicity of Python with the speed of C++, it is a promising option for scientific and numerical computing. The syntax of Julia is meant to be recognizable to users of R and Python, which lowers the entrance barrier. It can be readily integrated into current AI workflows by quickly calling Python and C libraries.

To sum up, the fundamentals of programming languages used in artificial intelligence cover a variety of instruments and functionalities that address different facets of AI creation. Python is a preferred language among many AI practitioners because of its adaptability, robust library support, and user-friendliness. R is the best choice for data-centric AI applications because it has unmatched statistical analysis and visualization capabilities. Java and C++ offer the performance and scalability required for large-scale and performance-critical AI systems. Programming for artificial intelligence may change in the future because of the performance and ease of use offered by emerging languages like Julia.

Overview of popular AI frameworks and libraries (TensorFlow, PyTorch, etc.)

Over the past ten years, there has been a significant advancement in artificial intelligence (AI), primarily due to the development of solid frameworks and libraries that make it easier to create and implement sophisticated AI models. TensorFlow and PyTorch are two of the most well-known and often utilized frameworks, each with unique features and benefits that meet various demands and tastes within the AI community.

Google Brain created the open-source deep learning framework TensorFlow, which is now widely used in academic and commercial applications. It was intended to be incredibly scalable and versatile, functioning on various hardware, including mobile devices and massively dispersed systems. The fundamental power of TensorFlow is its capacity to create and work with computational graphs, which show how data flows through various processes. This graph-based method makes it possible to optimize and deploy models efficiently, which is especially useful in production scenarios where scalability and efficiency are critical. Many tools and frameworks, including TensorBoard for visualization, TensorFlow Lite for mobile and embedded devices, and TensorFlow Serving for model deployment in a production environment, are all part of the TensorFlow ecosystem.

However, PyTorch—which Facebook's AI Research lab created—has become incredibly popular because of its dynamic computational graph, which provides more versatility and user-friendliness than TensorFlow's static graph method. PyTorch's dynamic nature makes it easier to debug and experiment, which is why research and development settings like it. Because PyTorch's design closely resembles ordinary Python code, it is easier for new users to get started because it emphasizes readability and simplicity. In addition, the framework has robust documentation and community, offering a wealth of tools for troubleshooting and learning. PyTorch is a flexible option for a range of AI applications because its ecosystem contains libraries for computer vision, audio processing, and natural language processing like torch text, touch audio and torch-vision. Additionally, PyTorch's connection with Open Neural Network

Keras, another notable AI framework, was originally designed as a high-level application programming interface for creating and refining deep learning models. Initially a stand-alone library, Keras has since been integrated into TensorFlow as the standard high-level API, simplifying the process of building neural networks. Keras allows users to prototype rapidly and effectively by abstracting away a large portion of the complexity associated with defining and training models.

The Berkeley Vision and Learning Center created Caffe, a deep learning framework emphasizing speed and modularity. It excels at computer vision tasks and is renowned for effectively using convolutional neural networks (CNNs). Caffe's model zoo minimizes the time and computing resources needed to create models from the start by offering a library of pre-trained models readily adjusted for particular tasks. Despite its advantages, more adaptable frameworks like TensorFlow and PyTorch, which provide more support for a broader range of neural network types and applications, have boosted the popularity of Caffe.

In conclusion, a wide range of AI frameworks and libraries are available, providing tools for all stages of AI development, from large-scale production deployment to research and experimentation. The two most popular frameworks are TensorFlow and PyTorch, each with special scalability, adaptability, and user-friendliness advantages. While Caffe and MXNet offer specific skills for computer vision and distributed computing, respectively, Keras provides an intuitive interface for quick prototyping. One essential tool for traditional machine learning tasks is still scikit-learn.

Setting up the development environment

Any software project must start with setting up a development environment, especially for those working in machine learning and artificial intelligence (ML). This procedure entails setting the required software, tools, and dependencies to facilitate practical application development, testing, and deployment. A well-structured development environment can significantly increase output, improve workflows, and lower the risk of errors and compatibility problems.

First things first, making the proper hardware selection is crucial. This usually entails having a computer with a powerful processor, lots of RAM, and, if possible, a dedicated Graphics Processing Unit (GPU) for AI and ML applications. GPUs are especially crucial for training deep learning models because they are more effective than conventional CPUs at handling the massively parallel computations needed for these tasks. Because they work with well-known deep learning frameworks like TensorFlow and PyTorch, which support CUDA, Nvidia's parallel computing platform, Nvidia GPUs are frequently chosen.

Selecting an operating system comes next after the hardware is installed. Any central operating system, such as Windows, macOS, and Linux, can be used to construct AI. However, many developers prefer Linux because of its adaptability, solid command-line interface, and interoperability with open-source tools. Within the AI community, distributions like Ubuntu and CentOS are very well-liked.

Once the operating system is configured, it is strongly advised to install package management. Software package dependencies and their installation, updates, and management are made more accessible by package managers. Common Linux commands include `yum` or `dnf} (for Red Hat-based systems like CentOS) and `apt} (for Debian-based systems like Ubuntu). Homebrew is a well-liked package manager for macOS, while Windows users frequently use Chocolatey.

Installing a version control system is the next crucial step; the most popular is Git. Git enables developers to manage multiple project versions, collaborate with others, and keep track of changes made to their code. A repository hosting account on Bitbucket, GitLab, or GitHub offers a platform for remote collaboration and continuous integration.

Selecting an integrated development environment (IDE) or code editor is also crucial. For AI and ML applications, IDEs like PyCharm, Jupyter Notebook, and Visual Studio Code are common choices. JetBrains' PyCharm provides extensive support for Python, including debugging, code completion, and integration with other frameworks and tools. Because it enables developers to integrate code, text, and visuals in a single document—a feature beneficial for exploratory data analysis and sharing results—Jupyter Notebook is a popular tool for interactive computing. Microsoft's Visual Studio Code is a lightweight and adaptable editor that supports many extensions, such as Jupyter and Python, to improve its capabilities for AI development.

Since Python is the most widely used programming language in AI and ML, updating the most recent version is essential. Setting up a virtual environment manager (such as `venv} or Conda) is necessary in addition to Python. With virtual environments, developers can establish segregated areas for their projects, preventing dependencies between them from interfering. In particular, Conda is a potent tool that supports numerous languages and is capable of managing environments and packages.

The next step after installing Python is to install the necessary frameworks and libraries. Libraries like NumPy, Pandas, and Scikit-learn are fundamental to machine learning. Large multi-dimensional arrays and matrices are supported by NumPy, which also offers several mathematical operations that can be performed on these arrays. Pandas provides the data structures and methods required to easily handle structured data, making it an essential tool for data analysis and manipulation. A vast collection of traditional machine learning tools and methods may be found in Scikit-learn.

Installing TensorFlow and PyTorch is essential for deep learning. The two most popular deep learning frameworks are TensorFlow (created by Google) and PyTorch (developed by Facebook), each with advantages and support from the community. Installing these libraries can be done through Conda or Pip, the package manager for Python. TensorFlow can also be used with Keras, which offers a high-level API for creating neural networks to streamline the model-building process.

An additional critical component of AI development is data visualization. For this, libraries like Matplotlib, Seaborn, and Plotly are frequently used. A flexible charting library that offers a great deal of control over plot appearance is Matplotlib. Seaborn is a higher-level interface for visually appealing statistical visualizations built on Matplotlib. Interactive visuals, which are especially helpful for presenting data insights, are made possible by Plotly.

AI initiatives frequently need databases, particularly those involving massive datasets. NoSQL databases like MongoDB are appropriate for unstructured or semi-structured data, while SQL databases like PostgreSQL and MySQL are frequently used for structured data. Installing and configuring these databases and learning how to use Python libraries like PyMongo for MongoDB and SQLAlchemy for SQL databases to communicate with them is crucial.

Lastly, the development workflow can be substantially improved by using continuous integration/deployment (CI/CD) and version control technologies. Platforms such as GitHub Actions, Travis CI, and Jenkins make automated testing and deployment possible. This guarantees that applications can be consistently released to production environments and that code changes do not introduce defects.

In conclusion, several essential tasks are involved in setting up an environment for AI and ML development, from choosing the appropriate hardware and operating system to installing the required tools and applications. In addition to increasing productivity, an adequately set environment guarantees a seamless, effective, and scalable development process. By following these steps, developers can lay a solid basis for their AI projects and ensure successful development and deployment.

CHAPTER III

Data Collection and Preparation

Importance of data in AI

It is impossible to exaggerate the significance of data in artificial intelligence (AI). AI systems rely heavily on data, essential to their creation, implementation, and overall efficacy. AI algorithms could not learn anything from a lack of data, preventing these systems from carrying out valuable functions. AI relies extensively on data for training, validating, and improving models in various fields, including computer vision, machine learning, and natural language processing.

Machine learning, a branch of AI that entails developing algorithms to learn from and make predictions or judgments based on data, is the fundamental component of artificial intelligence. Large volumes of data are needed for machine learning models to train efficiently, regardless of the model type—supervised, unsupervised, or reinforcement learning. Labeled datasets are necessary, for example, in supervised learning to educate models to identify patterns and generate precise predictions.

An important factor in determining how well AI systems work is the quality and quantity of data. Better model performance results from having clean, well-labeled data that faithfully captures the real-world environment in which the AI is intended to function. However, low-quality data might lead to biased, erroneous, or untrustworthy models. Cleaning, normalization, and augmentation are data preparation techniques essential to preparing raw data for use in AI models.

The quantity of data is just as crucial as the quality. Big datasets offer a wealth of data that enables AI algorithms to discover more complex links and patterns. Large volumes of data are required for complicated tasks like computer vision and natural language processing to capture the subtleties and variety of language and visual information. For example, in natural language processing, large text corpora covering a range of situations, languages, and dialects are needed to train a model to comprehend and produce human language.

Diversity of data is also essential for avoiding bias in AI systems. When training data does not represent the total population or situation the model is used with, bias in artificial intelligence can occur. This might result in models that generate biased results and perpetuate inequality by performing well on some data subsets but poorly on others. Diversity in the training data for AI models reduces prejudice and creates more equal and just AI systems.

Large-scale, high-quality datasets' accessibility has been crucial to the development of artificial intelligence. Researchers and developers may now train and assess AI models with substantial resources thanks to publicly available datasets like the UCI Machine Learning Repository for various tasks, the Common Crawl corpus for language models, and ImageNet for image identification. These datasets act as standard benchmarks, stimulating competition and creativity within the AI community and expanding the capabilities of AI systems.

To sum up, data is the basis of artificial intelligence and powers AI systems' creation, verification, and ongoing enhancement. Data type, volume, and diversity directly impact AI model performance and fairness. Publicly available datasets have accelerated advances in the field, and continuing data gathering and model retraining are necessary to keep AI systems relevant and efficient. The importance of data will only increase as AI develops, highlighting the necessity of sound data governance and ethical data practices to utilize AI while protecting ethical norms and privacy fully.

Sources of data: Public datasets, data scraping, APIs

Artificial intelligence (AI) and machine learning (ML) rely heavily on data that comes from a wide variety of sources. The most critical data sources include APIs, data scraping, and publicly available databases. Every one of these sources adds unique benefits and difficulties to the varied field of data collection that is necessary for creating AI models that work.

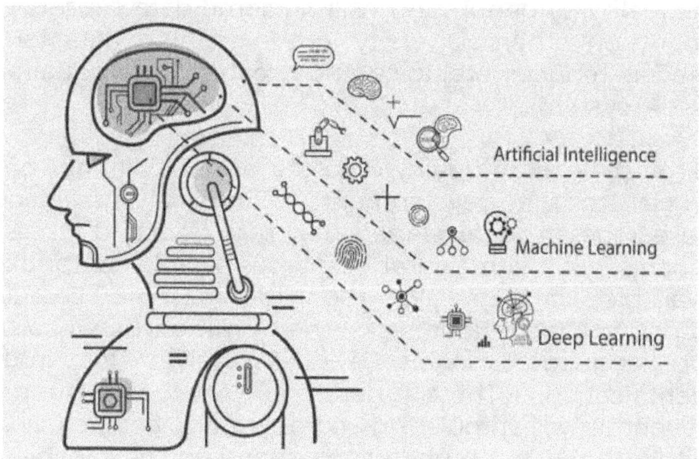

One essential and critical source of data for AI and ML initiatives is public datasets. To promote innovation, research, and development across various sectors, governments, corporations, and research institutes make these datasets available frequently at no cost. There are many types of public datasets, such as unstructured, semi-structured, and structured data. They cover various social sciences, healthcare, finance, and transportation topics. The ImageNet dataset, which has millions of tagged photos and is widely utilized in computer vision research, is among the most well-known public datasets. Another essential resource is the UCI Machine Learning Repository, which provides datasets for various machine-learning tasks, including regression, clustering, and classification. In addition, a wealth of statistics about economics, ecology, demography, and other subjects can be accessed through government websites such as data.gov in the United States.

Public datasets have significantly contributed to advancing AI research and development. Researchers and developers can train, test, and compare their models using these datasets, which offer a standard baseline. Within the AI community, benchmarking makes experiment reproducibility and result sharing easier. Furthermore, by granting equitable access to data, public datasets contribute to the democratization of AI by enabling independent researchers and smaller businesses to engage in AI innovation without investing significant resources in gathering and curating data.

A necessary additional means of gathering data is data scraping, sometimes called web scraping. Through the use of this technology, data is extracted from websites and formatted so that it can be used for analysis and training models. Python modules and technologies like BeautifulSoup, Scrapy, and Selenium can be used to automate data scraping. With these tools, developers can browse websites programmatically, get pertinent data, and store it in files or databases for later processing. When real-time data is needed or when some datasets are not publically accessible, data scraping can be especially helpful. For competitive analysis or recommendation systems, for instance, data on product prices, ratings, and availability can be obtained by scraping e-commerce websites. Similarly, social media platform scraping can reveal information on popular topics, sentiment analysis, and user activity.

However, there are difficulties and moral issues with data scraping. Terms of service on websites frequently prohibit automated data extraction; breaking these rules may have legal repercussions. Furthermore, websites may experience considerable load times due to data scraping, which could interfere with regular operations. Respecting website standards, avoiding unnecessary requests, and ensuring the extracted data is utilized appropriately and by applicable laws, such as the General Data Protection Regulation (GDPR), are all part of ethical data scraping procedures.

Application Programming Interfaces, or APIs, are yet another crucial data source. Developers can gain standardized and controlled access to data and services other software applications offer through APIs. Numerous companies, including internet behemoths like Google, Facebook, Twitter, and Amazon, provide APIs that let users access their enormous data archives. Developers can access tweets, user profiles, and trends through the Twitter API for sentiment analysis, social network analysis, and real-time event detection. Similarly, apps that offer location-based services, route planning, and spatial analysis can benefit from the geolocation data provided by the Google Maps API.

When compared to data scraping, APIs have many benefits. They offer a more dependable and lawful means of obtaining data, and they frequently come with assistance and documentation to help developers incorporate them into their apps. Real-time data access is another benefit of APIs, which is essential for programs like news aggregators, financial trading platforms, and weather forecasting systems that depend on current data. Furthermore, compared to data scraping, APIs usually provide more organized and clean data, which minimizes the need for intensive data preprocessing.

However, there are restrictions associated with using APIs. Utilization restrictions and authentication requirements are common in APIs, which can limit the volume of data that can be accessed and the frequency of queries. Large-scale data collection may become costly when using certain APIs, with use-based fees that increase with usage. Furthermore, depending on third-party APIs may result in dependencies and hazards if the API provider updates the API, discontinues it entirely, or changes their terms of service.

To sum up, many different data sources are available for AI and ML projects, each with unique advantages and difficulties. The development of artificial intelligence is greatly aided by public datasets, which offer standardized and easily accessible data for research and benchmarking. When particular datasets are unavailable, data scraping makes it possible to collect data from websites, but it comes with ethical and legal ramifications that must be carefully considered. APIs enhance real-time applications and ease the load of data preprocessing by providing an organized and frequently more dependable method of accessing data. Gaining the information required to create robust and influential AI models requires understanding various sources and their unique features.

Data cleaning and preprocessing techniques

Preprocessing and data cleaning are essential phases in the data science pipeline that guarantee the accuracy and consistency of the data used in machine learning (ML) and artificial intelligence (AI) models. Building accurate and dependable models requires high-quality data, and the cleaning and preprocessing steps take care of problems like noise, missing values, format errors, and inconsistencies. Converting unprocessed data into a format appropriate for analysis and modeling, these procedures help to enhance the functionality of artificial intelligence (AI) systems.

Data cleaning is known as finding and fixing mistakes and inconsistencies in the dataset. Dealing with missing values is one of the most frequent problems in data cleaning. Several factors, including mistakes made during data collecting, broken equipment, or human error, might result in missing data. Missing values can be handled in a few different ways. Eliminating records with missing values is one method, but this might result in a significant data loss, mainly if missing values are shared. Imputation of missing values is an additional method in which approximate values are used instead of missing entries. Simple techniques such as mean, median, or mode imputation substitute the column's mean, median, or mode for the missing value.

Another crucial component of data cleansing is the identification and handling of outliers. Data points significantly differing from the rest are called outliers and may result from mistakes or fundamental changes. One can identify outliers using statistical techniques like Z-scores and the IQR (Interquartile Range) approach. Outliers can be eliminated or altered once they have been identified. Eliminating anomalies has the potential to decrease noise and enhance the precision of the model; nevertheless, caution must be exercised to prevent the discarding of absolute deviations.

Resolving mistakes and inconsistencies within the dataset is another aspect of data cleansing. This can involve eliminating duplications, fixing typos, and standardizing formats. For example, standardizing date formats to a single format assures consistency when there are variations in the date formats inside the dataset. Similar labeling differences may exist for categorical data; for example, "Male" and "M" may indicate the same category; these label variations must be standardized. Duplicate records must be found and eliminated since they can exaggerate the importance of particular data items.

Following data cleaning, preparation procedures are carried out to prepare the data for modeling. Normalization or standardization of data is an essential preprocessing technique. While standardization changes the data to have a mean of 0 and a standard deviation of 1, normalization entails scaling the data to a given range, typically between 0 and 1. These methods are crucial for distance-calculating algorithms like support vector machines (SVM) and k-nearest neighbors (KNN). All features contribute equally to the model when the data is normalized or standardized, which keeps features with more comprehensive ranges from disproportionately affecting the outcomes.

Feature engineering is an essential preprocessing procedure that enhances model performance by generating additional features from preexisting data. This can involve feature selection, which selects the most pertinent features for modeling, and feature extraction, which extracts relevant information from raw data. Dimensionality reduction can be achieved by applying principle component analysis (PCA), which converts high-dimensional data into a lower-dimensional space while preserving most of the variation. This lessens the chance of overfitting and reduces computing complexity.

An essential aspect of data preparation is handling categorical data. Most machine learning methods require converting categorical data, such as labels or categories, into numerical form. Techniques like label encoding, in which each category is given a unique integer, and one-hot encoding, in which a binary vector represents each category, can be used to accomplish this. When there is no ordinal relationship between categories, one-hot encoding is most helpful; however, label encoding can be applied when there is.

Preprocessing involves using data transformation techniques, such as binning, polynomial transformation, and log transformation, to improve the data's eligibility for modeling. When dealing with skewed data, log transformation can help to enhance distributions' symmetry. Using polynomial transformation, which can help capture non-linear interactions, new features are created by elevating current features to power. Binning is a technique that helps streamline the modeling process and lessen the effect of noise by turning continuous data into discrete intervals.

Data augmentation is another crucial preprocessing step, particularly in domains where labeled data might be complex, such as computer vision and natural language processing. The size of the training dataset is artificially increased via data augmentation techniques, which include noise addition and synonym substitution for text and rotation, scaling, and flipping for images. Exposing the model to a more excellent range of circumstances enhances its robustness and generalization.

Beyond the initial cleaning and preprocessing, ensuring data consistency and integrity is ongoing. Finding and fixing any problems that develop during data gathering and processing entails routine validation and monitoring. Data quality may be sustained over time using automated data validation procedures and thorough documentation.

To sum up, preprocessing and data cleaning are essential phases in the AI and ML pipeline that turn unprocessed data into a format that can be used for modeling and analysis. These procedures improve the data by normalizing, feature engineering, and transforming while addressing missing values, outliers, inconsistencies, and formatting mistakes. High-quality data is ensured by efficient data cleaning and preprocessing, which produces more accurate, dependable, and broadly applicable models. Vigorous data cleaning and preprocessing techniques are becoming more and more necessary as the value of data in AI grows, making them fundamental competencies for any data scientist or AI practitioner.

Handling missing data and data augmentation

In data science and machine learning, handling missing data and augmentation is crucial for maintaining the accuracy and resilience of models. While data augmentation, which is especially useful in domains like computer vision and natural language processing, expands the quantity and variability of datasets, missing data handling takes care of incomplete datasets.

Missing data is a prevalent problem in datasets and can arise from several sources, including incorrect data input, broken equipment, and survey non-responses. Missing data can cause skewed estimates, diminished statistical power, and erroneous models. Thus, one of the most critical steps in the data preprocessing stage is addressing missing data. Missing data can be handled in several ways, each with benefits and disadvantages.

Deletion is a straightforward technique to deal with missing data; it entails deleting records or variables with missing values. Although this method is simple, it can result in a significant loss of data, mainly if there are a lot of missing entries. Only when there is a negligible percentage of missing data, and the remaining data still reflects the entire dataset, is deletion feasible. Listwise and pairwise deletion are the two primary forms.

A more complex technique is imputation, which replaces missing values with estimates. Simple imputation methods involve substituting the corresponding feature's mean, median, or mode for any missing values. Although these techniques are simple to use, they can potentially reduce data variability, which could result in understated standard errors. More sophisticated imputation methods use algorithms that consider other available data to forecast missing numbers. Regression imputation is the process of utilizing a regression model that has been trained on the observable data to estimate the missing value. The values of the closest neighbors are used in K-nearest neighbors (KNN) imputation to impute the missing value. A more reliable method is called multiple imputation, which entails generating many imputed datasets, examining each independently, and then merging the findings.

Using machine learning algorithms—which are naturally capable of handling missing values—is another method for dealing with missing data. Specific algorithms, such as random forests and decision trees, can handle missing data by employing the median of nearby values or surrogate splits. These algorithms may be helpful when imputation or deletion techniques are inadequate or inducing bias.

Contrarily, data augmentation makes up for the lack of available data by intentionally expanding and diversifying the training dataset. This method is beneficial in domains like computer vision and natural language processing, where obtaining sizable, labeled datasets can be challenging. Data augmentation increases resilience, minimizes overfitting, and improves model generalization of machine learning models by producing more training samples.

Data augmentation methods in computer vision involve rotation, scaling, translation, and flipping transformations. Modifying the original photos produces new ones, giving the model a wider variety of examples to work with. For example, a small amount of image rotation can train the model to identify items in any direction. Similarly, photos can be translated and scaled to represent various locations and distances, strengthening the model's resistance to changes in the input data. In computer vision, advanced augmentation techniques include cutoff, which obscures random areas of an image to encourage the model to focus on less noticeable aspects, and color jittering, which dynamically modifies the brightness, contrast, and saturation of images.

Data augmentation approaches in natural language processing generate new text data while maintaining the original meaning. Substituting substitutes for words in a sentence is a widespread technique. This method aids in the model's comprehension of various approaches to represent the same idea. Back-translation is another method that involves translating a sentence into another language and then returning to the original. This process produces new sentences with marginally different language and structure. Additional ways to incorporate variety into the text input and improve model generalization include random word substitutions, deletions, and insertions inside sentences.

Time-series data can also benefit from data augmentation, as new sequences can be produced by applying methods like time warping, scaling, and jittering. Scaling modifies the time series' amplitude, whereas jittering introduces tiny random noise to the data points. Time warping entails stretching or compressing the time gaps between data points to simulate various temporal patterns.

Even though data augmentation has many advantages, it is crucial to properly plan augmentation procedures to guarantee that the generated data is realistic and pertinent to the issue at hand. Noise can be introduced, and model performance can be decreased by over-augmentation or improper transformations. Thus, for efficient data augmentation, it is essential to comprehend the domain-specific features and limitations.

In summary, data augmentation and handling are essential steps in the data science and machine learning process. The quality and dependability of the dataset are guaranteed by appropriately handling missing data using imputation, deletion, or algorithm-specific techniques. By intentionally expanding the quantity and variety of the dataset, data augmentation enhances the generalization and resilience of the model. Both methods emphasize the significance of careful data pretreatment in development and are necessary for creating precise and efficient AI models. For those working in data science and machine learning, knowing these methods will continue to be essential as the value of data increases.

CHAPTER IV

Building Machine Learning Models

Supervised vs. Unsupervised learning

The two main paradigms in machine learning are supervised and unsupervised learning, each with its applications, difficulties, and methods. It is essential to comprehend how these two methods differ in choosing the proper techniques and algorithms for particular jobs.

An algorithm is trained on a labeled dataset in supervised learning, a kind of machine learning. Each data point in this scenario is associated with an output label, and the algorithm is trained to transfer the input data to the appropriate output. To learn, one must minimize a loss function that calculates the discrepancy between the actual labels and the expected outputs. Regression and classification are the two primary subcategories of supervised learning.

When the output variable is categorical, classification is applied. The algorithm gains the ability to classify input data into several predetermined groups. For example, in picture recognition, a classification algorithm can be trained to distinguish between distinct objects such as cats, dogs, and cars. Neural networks, decision trees, random forests, logistic regression, and support vector machines are some popular classification techniques. These models' performance is usually assessed using F1-score, accuracy, precision, and recall measures.

Conversely, when the output variable is continuous, regression is employed. Predicting a numerical number from the incoming data is the aim. Regression models, for instance, can forecast home values depending on characteristics like size, location, and number of bedrooms. The linear, polynomial, ridge, and lasso regression methods are examples of standard regression algorithms. Metrics like R-squared, mean absolute error (MAE) and mean squared error (MSE) are frequently used to evaluate the effectiveness of regression models.

Supervised learning offers various advantages, including its ability to provide accurate predictions and applicability to various real issues. It does, however, have certain restrictions. The requirement for vast quantities of labeled data, which can be costly and time-consuming to collect, is one of the main obstacles. Furthermore, overfitting—a condition in which a model performs well on training data but badly on fresh, untested data—can affect supervised learning methods. Cross-validation and regularization strategies are frequently employed to reduce overfitting.

In contrast, unsupervised learning involves training an algorithm on a dataset without labeled outputs. Finding hidden structures or patterns in the data is the aim. Unsupervised learning can be broadly divided into clustering and dimensionality reduction.

The clustering method involves assembling comparable data items according to their shared characteristics. When data points in a cluster are more similar to one another than they are to those in other clusters, the algorithm finds clusters in the data. Standard clustering techniques include k-means clustering, hierarchical clustering, and DBSCAN (Density-Based Spatial Clustering of Applications with Noise). Clustering has various uses, including customer segmentation, anomaly detection, and image compression. Unlike supervised learning, no predetermined labels evaluate clustering performance directly. Thus, metrics like silhouette score, Davies-Bouldin index, and the elbow technique are used to analyze the quality of the clusters.

Dimensionality reduction includes lowering the number of characteristics in a dataset while keeping as much information as possible. This is particularly beneficial for visualizing high-dimensional data and enhancing machine learning systems' effectiveness. Principal component analysis (PCA) and t-distributed stochastic neighbor embedding (t-SNE) extensively use dimensionality reduction techniques. PCA turns the original features into a new set of uncorrelated characteristics called principal components, which capture the most variance in the data. t-SNE, on the other hand, is a nonlinear approach that is particularly good for visualizing complicated datasets in two or three dimensions.

Unsupervised learning is advantageous because it may work with unlabeled data, which is typically more readily available than labeled data. It is also beneficial for exploratory data analysis, helping to find hidden structures and relationships within the data. Unsupervised learning does present a unique set of difficulties, though. One fundamental problem is the difficulty in analyzing the outcomes, as there are no ground truth labels to compare against. Furthermore, the choice of parameters and the initial conditions impact the performance of unsupervised learning algorithms, resulting in unpredictability in the output.

Depending on the particular issue at hand and the data that are accessible, either supervised or unsupervised learning should be used. Supervised learning is the best method when accurate prediction is the aim, and there is a precise mapping between input data and output labels. Applications like spam detection, picture classification, and medical diagnostics extensively use it. On the other hand, unsupervised learning works well for finding hidden patterns, data compression, and exploratory analysis. Applications such as market basket analysis, customer purchasing behavior clustering, and de-dimensionalizing gene expression data for bioinformatics are among its many uses.

In conclusion, there are two main methods in machine learning—supervised and unsupervised—each with different applications and techniques. For classification and regression problems, supervised learning uses labeled data to train models, which yields correct predictions but necessitates large, labeled datasets. On the other hand, unsupervised learning is helpful for exploratory analysis in scenarios where labeled data is limited because it uses unlabeled data to reveal latent patterns and structures. It is crucial to comprehend the distinctions between these two paradigms to choose the proper methods and complete machine learning projects. As the field progresses, the merger of supervised and unsupervised methods, coupled with advancements in semi-supervised and reinforcement learning, will further expand the possibilities and applications of machine learning.

Regression, classification, clustering algorithms

The fundamental machine learning tools are clustering, regression, and classification algorithms; each has a specific use. These algorithms find patterns, forecast outcomes, and model relationships within data, leading to several theoretical and practical developments.

Using input feature-based regression, one may forecast continuous outcomes. Fitting a linear equation to the observed data allows linear regression, one of the most straightforward and popular regression procedures, to represent the connection between a dependent variable and one or more independent variables. Using the least squares method, the main objective is to reduce the total of the squared discrepancies between the observed and predicted values. Since linear regression is simple to understand and apply, it is frequently used as the foundation for regression problems. Nonetheless, it presupposes a linear correlation across variables, which could not consistently hold in actuality.

Polynomial regression incorporates polynomial terms of the independent variables into linear regression to handle non-linear correlations. More complicated curves can be modeled thanks to this, but overfitting may result if the polynomial degree is too high. Regularized linear regression versions, such as ridge regression and Lasso regression, add penalties for significant coefficients to avoid overfitting and enhance the model's generalization ability to new data. Whereas Lasso regression uses L1 regularization, which penalizes the sum of the absolute values of the coefficients, Ridge regression uses L2 regularization, which penalizes the sum of the squared calculations. Combining L1 and L2 regularization, Elastic Net provides a well-rounded strategy that may be useful in some circumstances.

In contrast, classification algorithms are intended to forecast events that fall into specific categories. Despite its name, logistic regression is a well-liked classification approach that uses a logistic function to model the probability of a binary result. It converts the input features' linear combination into a probability score, which is then translated, depending on a threshold, to one of the two classes. Logistic regression is an extensively used technique because of its ease of use, interpretability, and efficiency in binary classification tasks. Extensions like the one-vs-rest method or multinomial logistic regression can be used for multi-class classification.

Another popular categorization algorithm is decision trees. They created a structure like a tree by iteratively dividing the data into subsets according to the most crucial property at each node. The path from the root to the leaf node indicates a decision rule, and each leaf node represents a class label. Decision trees handle both category and numerical data and are straightforward to interpret. Nevertheless, they are frequently overfit the training set, which results in subpar generalization on fresh data. This problem is addressed by ensemble techniques such as Random Forests and Gradient Boosting, which combine several decision trees to increase robustness and accuracy.

Robust classification techniques called Support Vector Machines (SVM) seek to identify the ideal hyperplane that divides data points into various classes. By maximizing the space between the data points and the hyperplane, support vector machines (SVMs) provide a strong classification border. SVMs use kernel functions, like the radial basis function (RBF) kernel or the polynomial kernel, to transform non-linear data into a higher-dimensional space where it can be separated linearly. SVMs are renowned for their accuracy and versatility and work well in high-dimensional areas.

In recent years, neural networks have transformed categorization tasks and intense learning models. A neural network comprises layers of connected neurons that alter the incoming data somehow. Deep neural networks—with several hidden layers—are well-suited for tasks like speech identification, image recognition, and natural language processing because they can learn intricate representations and patterns. Convolutional neural networks (CNNs) are specialized neural networks that use convolutional layers to capture spatial hierarchies to analyze grid-like data, such as photographs. To handle sequential input, like text or time series, recurrent neural networks (RNNs) use loops that maintain information throughout time steps.

In unsupervised learning, clustering algorithms group comparable data points according to their intrinsic structure instead of regression and classification. One of the most straightforward and often used clustering methods is K-means clustering. By minimizing the sum of squared distances between data points and the cluster centroids that correspond to them, it divides the data into k clusters. The algorithm changes the centroids based on the mean of the allocated points after iteratively assigning data points to the closest centroid. K-means is a computationally efficient method, although it depends on the initial centroidal positioning and requires the number of clusters to be specified beforehand.

By beginning with each data point as a separate cluster and merging the closest pairs (agglomerative clustering) or beginning with all the data points in a single cluster and recursively separating them (divisive clustering), hierarchical clustering creates a hierarchy of clusters. The outcome is a dendrogram, a diagram resembling a tree, and displaying the clusters' layered structure. Although complicated cluster structures can be captured by hierarchical clustering, which does not need pre-specifying the number of clusters, it is computationally costly for large datasets.

A density-based clustering algorithm called DBSCAN (Density-Based Spatial Clustering of Applications with Noise) clusters data points according to their density. It can discover clusters of any shape and defines clusters as dense regions of data points divided by regions of lesser density. DBSCAN can have trouble with different densities within the same dataset, but it is noise-resistant and doesn't require pre-specifying the number of clusters.

The machine learning toolkit comprises essential regression, classification, and clustering algorithms, each with a specific function. While clustering algorithms gather related data points without predetermined labels, regression algorithms predict continuous results, while classification algorithms predict categorical outcomes. Understanding these algorithms' capabilities, constraints, and suitable uses is essential for solving various machine-learning issues, such as categorizing data, forecasting numerical values, and detecting hidden patterns in unlabeled datasets.

Training and evaluating models

To create precise, effective, and dependable predictive systems, machine learning and artificial intelligence require the training and evaluation of models. This process has several essential steps, and each one is vital to the model's successful operation with real-world data. Gaining a deeper understanding of these stages might help you better understand machine learning's intricacies and the best methods for creating reliable models.

Preprocessing and data collecting are the first steps in the trip. The caliber and volume of accessible data heavily influence the model's performance. The data must encompass a broad range of scenarios the model may encounter and reflect the issue domain. Preprocessing includes resolving missing values, adjusting or scaling characteristics to provide uniformity, and cleaning the data to eliminate noise and inconsistencies. Preprocessing also involves the crucial feature engineering step involving variable creation, selection, and transformation.

The next stage after preparing the data is to choose an appropriate model. The type of task (classification, regression, clustering, etc.), the data's properties, and the application's particular needs all influence this decision. Neural networks, decision trees, support vector machines, linear regression, and ensemble techniques like random forests and gradient boosting machines are examples of standard models. Every model has advantages and disadvantages, and choosing one frequently requires balancing interpretability and complexity.

The preprocessed data must be fed into the selected algorithm to train the model to discover the underlying patterns. The process involves fine-tuning the model's parameters to minimize a loss function quantifying the discrepancy between the predicted and actual values. Methods like gradient descent are frequently employed for this kind of optimization. Monitoring the model's performance on a validation set in addition to the training data is crucial. When a model overfits—that is, performs well on training data but badly on unknown data—the validation set aids in identifying overfitting. By including a penalty for complexity in the loss function, regularization techniques like L1 and L2 regularization, dropout in neural networks, and pruning in decision trees can assist in reducing overfitting.

The model has to be evaluated to determine its performance after training. A different test set that wasn't used for training or validation must be employed to do this. The primary assessment criteria differ according to the nature of the issue. Metrics including accuracy, precision, recall, F1 score, and area under the receiver operating characteristic (ROC) curve are frequently employed for classification jobs. Metrics like mean absolute error, mean squared error, and R-squared are commonly used for regression tasks. These metrics offer a numerical assessment of the model's expected performance on fresh, untested data.

Cross-validation is a reliable model evaluation method, mainly for sparse data. It entails dividing the data into multiple subsets, using some subsets to train the model and the remaining ones to validate it. This process is performed several times to get a more accurate measure of the model's performance, with the average results. By ensuring that a specific train-test split does not bias the model and that it generalizes well to many data sets, cross-validation helps accomplish these two goals.

An analysis of errors and residuals is also a part of the model evaluation to determine where the model might be failing. Visual aids such as residual plots for regression and confusion matrices for classification help shed light on the many kinds of errors and their trends. Knowing these mistakes might help with future model improvement, including adjusting hyperparameters, picking alternative features, or switching to a different algorithm.

Not only are these technical elements essential, but practical considerations are even more so. Essential considerations include interpretability, scalability, and computational efficiency, particularly in real-world applications where models must process massive amounts of data quickly or offer justification for their predictions. Strategies including model quantization, model compression, and the usage of more comprehensible models like decision trees or linear models might be used to address these issues.

Ultimately, a model needs to be put into production after it has been trained and assessed. This entails incorporating the model into the working environment, ensuring it can process real-time data, and tracking its effectiveness over time. Since data distributions might alter and induce model erosion, ongoing observation is crucial. Maintaining the accuracy and dependability of the model requires regular retraining with fresh data and modifying it based on feedback and performance indicators.

Training and assessing models is complex and involves several factors, including data quality, model selection, training protocols, assessment criteria, and realistic deployment considerations. For models to be developed that are resilient and trustworthy in real-world applications, in addition to being accurate and efficient, each stage is essential. Any artificial intelligence and machine learning practitioner must comprehend and become proficient in this process.

Hyperparameter tuning and model optimization

The performance and effectiveness of predictive models are determined by hyperparameter tweaking and model optimization, which are essential components of the machine-learning workflow. Hyperparameters are predetermined and govern the learning process, unlike model parameters, which are discovered during training. Optimizing these hyperparameters can significantly improve a model's precision, effectiveness, and generalizability.

The model type being utilized determines the hyperparameters. Hyperparameters in a decision tree could be the criterion for splitting, the minimum number of samples needed to split a node, and the maximum depth of the tree. The learning rate, the number of hidden layers, the number of neurons per layer, and the kind of activation functions are examples of hyperparameters in neural networks. The selection of these hyperparameters can significantly impact the model's capacity to learn from data and generalize to new samples.

Grid search is one of the most used techniques for hyperparameter tweaking. Grid search entails giving each hyperparameter a range of potential values and then training and assessing the model for each conceivable combination of these values. This thorough search is time-consuming and computationally expensive, especially when dealing with many hyperparameters or massive datasets, but it guarantees the discovery of the ideal combination. Practitioners frequently employ a more narrowly defined subset of potential values based on domain expertise or exploratory testing to lessen this.

Random search is another well-liked technique that chooses a predetermined number of hyperparameter combinations at random for evaluation rather than thoroughly searching every combination. Since it frequently identifies good combinations more quickly than grid search, this method may be more effective in some situations. Because random search searches a more extensive range of values and is less prone to become trapped in less-than-ideal areas of the search space, studies have shown that it can be more effective than grid search.

Bayesian optimization provides a more advanced method by creating a probabilistic model of the objective function and utilizing it to determine which hyperparameters are most promising to test. To prevent local optima, this approach strikes a balance between exploration and exploitation, concentrating on regions of the search space that are most likely to produce better results while occasionally venturing into less promising areas. Especially for complicated models and massive datasets, Bayesian optimization is more efficient than grid and random search because it finds optimal or nearly ideal hyperparameters with fewer evaluations.

Another method that combines early halting and random search is called hyperband. With limited data, it evaluates many hyperparameter settings at first, then progressively focuses more resources on the configurations that show the most promise. This approach successfully cuts computing costs because it rapidly eliminates ineffective configurations and concentrates on those that function well.

Beyond these conventional approaches, automated machine learning (AutoML) frameworks have been developed due to machine learning developments. AutoML systems combine many search strategies and advanced techniques, such as ensemble methods and meta-learning, to automate optimizing models and fine-tuning hyperparameters. With the help of these technologies, creating high-performing models can be completed faster and with less experience, opening up advanced machine-learning techniques to a broader audience.

Model optimization entails enhancing different facets of the performance and efficiency of the model, going beyond hyperparameter adjustment. In this procedure, methods including regularization, optimization algorithms, feature extraction and selection, and regularization are essential. By minimizing overfitting and boosting generalization, feature selection helps improve model performance by locating and keeping the most pertinent features. Contrarily, feature extraction entails generating new features from existing ones to identify more intricate patterns and connections within the data.

By adding a penalty for high coefficients in the model, regularization approaches like L1 and L2 regularization prevent overfitting by discouraging too complex models. Dropout is a regularization strategy in neural networks that includes randomly discarding units during training. By preventing neurons from co-adapting, dropout improves network generalization.

Stochastic gradient descent (SGD) and its derivatives (e.g., Adam, RMSprop) are essential optimization methods for training models efficiently. Hyperparameters like learning rate and momentum can impact the performance of these algorithms, which iteratively update model parameters to minimize the loss function. Adaptive learning rate techniques can significantly enhance Convergence and model performance, which modify the learning rate during training in response to observed performance.

Additionally, ensemble approaches can improve the robustness and performance of the model by combining predictions from many models. By combining the advantages of several models, strategies like bagging, boosting, and stacking generate more reliable and accurate forecasts. In these approaches, hyperparameter adjustment is crucial to guarantee the optimal performance of both the individual and ensemble models.

Creating successful machine learning models requires both model optimization and hyperparameter tuning. They use various methods to maximize different parts of the model's performance and conduct a systematic search for the ideal hyperparameters. These operations necessitate striking a compromise between exhaustive search space exploration and computational efficiency, and improvements in automated procedures are opening up new avenues for these enhancements. Gaining proficiency in these areas is essential to creating models that work reliably, effectively, and accurately in practical settings.

CHAPTER V

Deep Learning and Neural Networks

Introduction to neural networks

Artificial intelligence and machine learning have undergone a revolutionary change thanks to neural networks, which provide previously unheard-of powers in data analysis, predictive modeling, and pattern identification. Neural networks, modeled after the architecture and operations of the human brain, are made up of layers of interconnected nodes, or neurons, that collaborate to process and learn from data. With an emphasis on their transformative power across multiple areas, this introduction seeks to give readers a thorough grasp of neural networks, including their construction, operation, and applications.

Although the idea of neural networks has been around since the 1940s, it hasn't been until recently that substantial developments and real-world uses have been made possible by growing processing power and the accessibility of massive datasets. An input layer, one or more hidden layers, and an output layer make up a neural network's fundamental components. There are many neurons in each layer, and every neuron in one layer is coupled to every other layer's neuron. These connections' corresponding weights are changed throughout training to reduce the error in the network's predictions.

Raw data, comprising text, graphics, and numerical values, is sent to the input layer. The buried layer neurons process this data by applying a weighted sum of their inputs, a bias term, and an activation function to each neuron. By adding non-linearity to the model, activation functions let the network recognize intricate patterns. The sigmoid rectified linear unit (ReLU) and hyperbolic tangent (tanh) are examples of standard activation functions. Depending on the application, the output layer generates a more complicated output, a single value in regression tasks, a probability distribution in classification activities, or both.

A neural network is trained by varying the weights and biases of its neurons to reduce the discrepancy between the goal values and the expected output. Usually, backpropagation is used with an optimization algorithm such as stochastic gradient descent (SGD) or one of its variations (e.g., Adam, RMSprop) to carry out this procedure. The network's prediction error is propagated backward through the layers during backpropagation, and the weights are adjusted to lower this error. Until the model's performance on a validation set stabilizes, a sign that it has discovered the underlying patterns in the data, the training procedure is repeated iteratively.

Neural networks can be generally classified into several varieties according to their use and architecture. The most basic type of neural networks are feedforward ones, in which there are no cycles in the connections between the neurons. These networks are extensively employed for tasks such as regression and image categorization. A specific feedforward network called a convolutional neural network (CNN) handles grid-like data, such as photographs. CNNs are very good at image and video identification tasks because they use convolutional layers to automatically and adaptively learn spatial hierarchies of information from input images.

On the other hand, recurrent neural networks (RNNs) use connections that create directed cycles to process sequential data. Because of their architecture, RNNs may retain a memory of past inputs, which makes them useful for applications like time series prediction, speech recognition, and language modeling. Traditional RNN training on lengthy sequences can be hampered by the vanishing gradient problem, which has led to the development of variants such as gated recurrent units (GRUs) and long short-term memory (LSTM).

The generative adversarial network (GAN), composed of a generator and a discriminator neural network, is another noteworthy kind. While the discriminator assesses the data's authenticity, the generator produces false data that replicates the original data. As a result of the two networks being trained concurrently in a competitive manner, incredibly realistic data is created. Applications for GANs include data augmentation, style transfer, and visual creation.

Numerous industries have seen advancements with the introduction of deep learning, which uses deep neural networks (networks with multiple layers). As evidenced by AlphaGo, deep learning models have surpassed humans in various tasks, including speech and picture recognition, natural language processing, and even playing strategic video games. Hardware advancements like graphics processing units (GPUs) and tensor processing units (TPUs), which offer the processing capacity needed to train big, complicated models, have significantly influenced these successes.

Neural networks are successful, but they also have several drawbacks. They need a lot of labeled data for training, which can be hard to come by and expensive. Deep network training also requires a lot of computing and can take a while. Additionally, there is a chance of overfitting, which occurs when a model works well with training data but needs to be better with untested data. Strategies including dropout, regularization, and data augmentation are applied to lessen this risk.

Furthermore, there is still much to learn about the interpretability and explainability of neural networks. In contrast to conventional machine learning models, neural networks are frequently viewed as "black boxes," making it challenging to comprehend how they make particular predictions. This lack of openness may provide challenges in vital applications like healthcare and finance, where comprehension of the need for decision-making is essential.

In conclusion, neural networks have revolutionized artificial intelligence by making it possible for machines to complete challenging tasks accurately. Thanks to their architecture, which was heavily influenced by the human brain, they can learn and generalize from data in previously unthinkable ways. The capabilities of neural networks are predicted to grow as research is conducted, and new methods are developed, opening up new avenues for application and potential in various fields.

Architecture of neural networks: Layers, neurons, activation functions

Neural network architecture is a unique and complex structure that emulates the human brain's learning and information-processing capabilities. It comprises layers, neurons, and activation functions that combine to convert input data into useful outputs. Understanding these elements and how they work together is essential to understanding how neural networks function and can be tailored for different activities.

The layers of a neural network form its fundamental structure. The network's building components, or layers, are organized sequentially to create a deep architecture that can recognize intricate patterns. Input, hidden, and output layers are the three primary categories of layers. The first layer to receive raw data is the input layer. Each neuron in the input layer represents a feature of the data, such as the values of pixels in an image or the attributes in a dataset.

The layers between the input and output layers are known as hidden layers. For the extraction and processing of features, these layers are essential. Neurons in each buried layer process the data gathered from the layer above to carry out calculations. Depending on the task's complexity and the neural network's architecture, there can be a significant variation in the number of hidden layers and neurons in each layer. Multiple hidden layers of deep neural networks are extreme because they can collect and represent complex patterns and relationships in the data.

The output layer, the last layer in the network, generates outputs or predictions based on the patterns it has learned. When doing classification tasks, each class may have a neuron in the output layer, and the output values indicate the likelihood that the input falls into each class. The output layer of regression tasks usually consists of a single neuron that produces a continuous result.

Neural networks' basic building blocks, neurons, are comparable to the nerve cells found in the human brain. Every neuron takes in information from the neurons in the layer above it, transforms it, and then sends the finished product to the neurons in the layer below it—the weights and bias of the neuron control this transition. The bias is an extra parameter that helps the model fit the data more accurately, whereas the weights dictate how strongly neurons link.

A neuron functions by adding the bias, computing the weighted total of its inputs, and then using an activation function. To add non-linearity to the network is the aim of the activation function. No matter how many layers a network has, it can only model linear relationships without non-linearity. Thanks to activation functions, neural networks can learn and represent intricate, non-linear mappings between inputs and outputs.

Neural networks frequently employ a variety of activation functions, each having unique properties and uses. When used for binary classification problems, the sigmoid activation function transfers the input values to a range between 0 and 1. Its training procedure is slowed down by the vanishing gradient problem, which occurs when gradients are minimal during backpropagation.

Like the sigmoid function, the hyperbolic tangent (tanh) activation function transfers input values to a range between -1 and 1. Because this function is zero-centered, training may proceed more quickly. However, it also has the issue of the disappearing gradient.

Because of its efficiency and simplicity, the rectified linear unit (ReLU) activation function has gained much popularity. If the input is positive, ReLU outputs the value directly; if not, it produces zero. This function reduces the vanishing gradient issue and speeds up training by permitting gradients to flow while the input is positive. Nevertheless, neurons may go dormant and produce zero in ReLU because of the dying ReLU problem. This problem is addressed by variants that allow tiny gradients when the input is negative, such as leaky ReLU and parametric ReLU.

Other activation functions include the swish function, a recent function that combines linear and non-linear behaviors and has shown promise in specific applications, and the softmax function, typically used in classification networks' output layer to convert raw output scores into probabilities.

The interaction between layers, neurons, and activation functions determines the neural network's ability to learn from data. The network modifies the neuronal weights and biases throughout training to reduce prediction error. An optimization technique, such as Adam or stochastic gradient descent (SGD), which iteratively adjusts the parameters based on the gradients of the loss function, serves as the basis for this adjustment.

Regularization methods like batch normalization and dropout are frequently applied to enhance the network's generalization performance. During training, dropout randomly deactivates a portion of the neurons, preventing overfitting by preventing the network from becoming overly dependent on any one neuron. Higher learning rates are possible, and the learning process is stabilized when each layer's inputs are normalized by batch normalization.

The nature of the task, the quantity and kind of data available, and the processing resources are only a few of the many variables that must be carefully considered while designing a neural network's architecture. Building efficient neural networks requires careful consideration of the network's depth and width, application of regularization techniques, and choice of appropriate activation functions.

In conclusion, layers, neurons, and activation functions make up the intricate structure that is neural network architecture. Every element is essential to the network's ability to learn from data and generate precise predictions. To create and refine neural networks for various uses, such as autonomous driving, image recognition, and natural language processing, it is essential to comprehend these components and how they interact. The capabilities and performance of neural networks are predicted to grow as research is conducted and new methods are developed, opening up even greater possibilities in various disciplines.

Convolutional Neural Networks (CNNs) and Recurrent Neural Networks (RNNs)

In deep learning, Convolutional Neural Networks (CNNs) and Recurrent Neural Networks (RNNs) are two well-known architectures intended to handle distinct kinds of data and tasks. Leveraging these architectural strengths across multiple areas requires understanding these designs, their unique features, and their applications.

The primary use of convolutional neural networks (CNNs) is processing grid-like input, including pictures and movies. By significantly enhancing the precision and effectiveness of tasks like picture classification, object identification, and image segmentation, they have completely transformed the field of computer vision. The convolutional layer, which uses a mathematical process known as convolution to extract spatial information from the input data, is the primary innovation in CNNs. Convolutional layers comprise several filters, also known as kernels, that move over the input data to multiply it element by element and then total the outputs. At various levels of abstraction, these filters can identify patterns such as edges, textures, and forms.

Many convolutional layers are found in a standard CNN design, followed by pooling and fully linked layers. By reducing the spatial dimensions of the feature maps, they are pooling layers like max pooling and average pooling help to lower the computational effort and manage overfitting. The final predictions are made by fully connected layers, which resemble those in conventional neural networks, after integrating the high-level characteristics that the convolutional layers have collected. CNNs have several advantages; one is their capacity to learn hierarchical representations, in which lower-level information is captured by the first layers and more complicated patterns are captured by the deeper layers.

CNNs frequently use activation functions such as ReLU (Rectified Linear Unit) to introduce non-linearity and aid in the network's learning of more complex functions. Additionally, regularization strategies like dropout enhance generalization by keeping the network from becoming overly dependent on any one neuron during training.

Conversely, Recurrent Neural Networks (RNNs) are perfect for applications like natural language processing, audio recognition, and time series prediction since they are specifically made to handle sequential input. RNNs consider the temporal dependencies in sequential data by keeping a hidden state updated at each time step, in contrast to CNNs, which assume the input data is independent and identically distributed.

The recurrent cell, the basic building block of an RNN, generates the output and the updated hidden state by using the input at the current time step and the secret state from the previous time step. Using this technique, RNNs can remember information from prior inputs and anticipate outcomes depending on the sequence's context. Standard RNNs, however, have difficulties such as the vanishing gradient problem, which makes it challenging to learn long-term dependencies since gradients used to update the network's weights diminish with time as they are backpropagated.

Advanced RNN variations, including Gated Recurrent Units (GRUs) and Long Short-Term Memory (LSTM) networks, have been created to address this problem. LSTMs introduce gates to control the flow of information, allowing memory cells to retain information for extended periods. The information to be added, removed, or output from the cell state is determined by these gates, which are the input gate, forget gate, and output gate. Compared to conventional RNNs, LSTMs are better able to capture long-range dependencies because of their structure.

The cell and hidden states are combined into a single state in GRUs, a condensed form of LSTMs requiring the update and reset gates. In several cases, GRUs have outperformed LSTMs with a more straightforward structure, frequently requiring less computing power.

Both CNNs and RNNs have a wide range of uses in various industries. CNNs are frequently employed in computer vision tasks, including object identification with frameworks like YOLO (You Only Look Once) and Faster R-CNN, picture segmentation with designs like U-Net and Mask R-CNN, and image classification with models like AlexNet, VGG, and ResNet. These applications achieve accuracy and robustness by utilizing CNN's hierarchical feature learning capabilities.

Natural language processing activities, including sentiment analysis, machine translation, and language modeling, are performed mainly by RNNs and their variants. For example, RNNs in language modeling can anticipate the following word in a sentence by considering the context given by the words that come before it. RNN-based encoder-decoder architectures, in which the encoder interprets the input sentence and produces the translated output sentence, have proven to be quite effective in machine translation. RNNs are also used by speech recognition systems to transcribe spoken language into text, utilizing their capacity to represent temporal dependencies.

In addition, hybrid architectures that combine RNNs and CNNs have been developed to tackle jobs that require both temporal and spatial input. CNNs help extract spatial characteristics from individual frames in video analysis, whereas RNNs are more suited for modeling the temporal dynamics between frames. With this combination, video content can be effectively analyzed for action detection and captioning.

In conclusion, there are two different but complementary methods for deep learning: convolutional neural networks (CNNs) and recurrent neural networks (RNNs). CNNs use convolutional layers to collect hierarchical features, which makes them excellent at processing spatial data, especially in computer vision applications. Because RNNs are built to handle sequential data, they work well on jobs with temporal dependencies, such as speech recognition and natural language processing. These architectures' capabilities have been further improved by advancements, such as LSTMs and GRUs for RNNs, which allow them to handle issues that are getting more complicated. The synergy between CNNs and RNNs is expected to open up new possibilities and applications across multiple areas as research progresses, propelling further developments in artificial intelligence.

Transfer learning and pre-trained models

Machine learning has revolutionized because of transfer learning and pre-trained models, which have significantly improved productivity, accuracy, and the capacity to handle challenging jobs with sparse data. The process of using a model created for one activity to serve as the foundation for another task is known as transfer learning. With this method, you can handle new and related issues more successfully by utilizing the information that a pre-trained model—typically trained on a large and diverse dataset—has acquired.

The premise that multiple machine learning tasks have common properties is the foundation of the transfer learning concept. For example, a model trained on a massive dataset such as ImageNet—which has millions of photos in thousands of categories—learns to recognize generic features like edges, textures, and forms in image identification. These characteristics are frequently helpful for a variety of different picture recognition tasks. We may use this acquired knowledge for a new goal, like identifying plant species or specific objects in medical photos, with much less data and computational work by employing a pre-trained model on ImageNet.

Transfer learning usually entails using an existing model that has already been trained and optimizing it for the new task-specific dataset. The pre-trained model's weights are adjusted during fine-tuning to suit the latest data better while preserving the valuable features discovered during the initial task. This method works exceptionally well with small new datasets since starting from scratch with a deep neural network will probably lead to overfitting and subpar generalization. Compared to training a model from scratch, we can get faster convergence and more excellent performance by starting with a pre-trained model.

Reducing the time and computational resources needed for training is one of the main benefits of transfer learning. Deep neural networks require significant processing power and time to train, especially ones with millions of parameters. By reusing the previously learned features, pre-trained models reduce this problem and need incremental training for the current task. Because of its effectiveness, transfer learning is especially beneficial for institutions and researchers with restricted access to large-scale computing resources.

Enhanced task performance with little labeled data is a noteworthy advantage of transfer learning. Significant annotated dataset acquisition can be costly and time-consuming, particularly in specialist fields like remote sensing or medical imaging. By utilizing the generalizable features discovered from larger datasets, transfer learning makes it possible to use smaller datasets more effectively. This method improves model performance and makes sophisticated machine-learning approaches more accessible, enabling smaller businesses and research groups to produce cutting-edge outcomes.

Transfer learning requires pre-trained models, of which a few have become well-known for their effectiveness and adaptability. Models like VGG, ResNet, Inception, and Efficient Net are commonly employed in computer vision. These models offer a solid basis for various image-related tasks because they have been pre-trained on large datasets such as ImageNet. For example, ResNet's novel residual connections enable the training of intense networks, capturing complex patterns and producing excellent results.

Pre-trained models like BERT (Bidirectional Encoder Representations from Transformers), GPT (Generative Pre-trained Transformer), and ELMo (Embeddings from Language Models) have revolutionized the field of natural language processing (NLP). Large text datasets are used to pre-train these models, which help them acquire rich language representations that can be optimized for various natural language processing (NLP) applications, such as sentiment analysis, question answering, and machine translation. For instance, BERT achieves state-of-the-art speed on numerous benchmarks by capturing bidirectional context using a transformer design.

In particular, introducing transformer models has completely changed NLP transfer learning. The transformer design overcomes the shortcomings of earlier models like RNNs and LSTMs by enabling the modeling of long-range dependencies in text through its self-attention mechanism. Large-scale pre-training for downstream applications can be harnessed through transfer learning, as demonstrated by models such as BERT and GPT, which have broken records in various NLP tasks.

Furthermore, transfer learning is not just used in vision and natural language processing (NLP); it can also be applied in other fields, including speech recognition, reinforcement learning, and even cross-modal tasks that involve different input sources. Large audio datasets are used by pre-trained speech recognition algorithms like DeepSpeech and wav2vec to enhance their performance on specific speech tasks. By transferring knowledge from previously acquired tasks, transfer learning in reinforcement learning helps expedite the training of agents in new settings.

Transfer learning has many benefits, but it also has some drawbacks. A significant obstacle is the possibility of negative transfer, in which the performance of the pre-trained model could be better due to poor alignment between its knowledge and the new task. Choosing a suitable pre-trained model and figuring out how much fine-tuning is needed are important choices that affect transfer learning outcomes. Further studies on transfer learning methods for tasks with significantly different domains or distributions from the pre-training data are also needed.

In conclusion, by enhancing effectiveness, performance, and accessibility, transfer learning and pre-trained models have significantly advanced the field of machine learning. Transfer learning makes advanced machine learning techniques more accessible by utilizing pre-existing knowledge by reducing the requirement for big datasets and substantial computer resources. The efficacy of this technique has been proven in a variety of domains by pre-trained models such as ResNet, BERT, and GPT, which have opened up new possibilities and set records in domains like computer vision and natural language processing. Research will have a more significant influence and advance machine learning as long as it addresses the issues and broadens the applications of transfer learning.

CHAPTER VI

Natural Language Processing (NLP)

Basics of NLP and its applications

The study of natural language interaction between computers and people is the focus of the artificial intelligence field known as natural language processing, or NLP. Enabling computers to comprehend, interpret, and produce meaningful and practical human language is the main objective of natural language processing (NLP). This field includes various activities and applications, including conversational bots, machine translation, text analysis, and sentiment detection. Knowing the fundamentals of NLP and its many uses will help you see how it affects our day-to-day activities and advances communication and technology.

Several basic tasks are at the heart of natural language processing (NLP), and they work together to enable a machine to process language. Tokenization, part-of-speech tagging, named entity recognition, parsing, and sentiment analysis are some of these activities. The process of tokenizing text involves dividing it into smaller pieces known as tokens, which can be individual words, phrases, or symbols. Since it enables the machine to process the material in digestible bits, this is the first stage in interpreting any text. Labeling each token with the appropriate part of speech—such as an adjective, verb, or noun—is known as part-of-speech tagging. This aids in comprehending the sentence's grammatical structure.

Named entity recognition (NER) recognizes and categorizes essential textual elements, including places, dates, names of individuals and organizations, and more.

Parsing, sometimes referred to as syntactic analysis, is dissecting a sentence's grammatical structure to determine the connections between its various parts. Determining the emotional tone of a text—whether it is favorable, harmful, or neutral—is another important task in sentiment analysis. These fundamental activities serve as the foundation for more intricate NLP applications.

Machine translation involves a computer translating speech or text between languages and is one of the most well-known uses of natural language processing (NLP). Early machine translation techniques were based on statistical methods and rule-based systems. Neural machine translation (NMT) models, on the other hand, have become more popular recently. NMT models leverage deep learning approaches to attain improved accuracy and fluency. Notable examples of NMT systems with much-enhanced language translation capabilities are Google Translate and Microsoft Translator.

Search engines and information retrieval are two critical areas where natural language processing is used. NLP techniques are used by search engines such as Google to interpret user queries and deliver relevant search results. These systems can provide more precise and valuable results by analyzing search queries' context and intent. NLP is also utilized in text summarizing, a process where algorithms produce summaries of lengthy papers while keeping the essential details. This is especially helpful for reading through lengthy texts fast, such as research papers, news stories, and court records.

Virtual assistants and chatbots are two more common uses of NLP. These apps, which include Google Assistant, Amazon's Alexa, and Apple's Siri, use natural language processing (NLP) to comprehend spoken or written questions and provide relevant answers. They can do many different things, such as answering general knowledge inquiries, creating reminders, and managing smart home appliances. To deliver fluid and engaging user experiences, these assistants take advantage of speech recognition, natural language production, and natural language understanding developments.

Sentiment analysis is extensively employed in customer feedback analysis and social media monitoring. Businesses examine comments, reviews, and postings on social media platforms to determine how the public feels about their goods, services, or brand. This process is known as sentiment analysis. This aids companies in gauging client happiness, seeing any problems, and refining their products in response to comments. Similarly, sentiment analysis is utilized in finance to forecast stock market movements and assess market sentiment from news items and social media conversations.

Natural language processing (NLP) has revolutionary uses in the medical area. Large volumes of unstructured text data, including clinical notes, patient histories, and diagnostic findings, are found in electronic health records, or EHRs. From these records, NLP algorithms can extract useful information to help with patient management, clinical decision-making, and medical research. NLP, for instance, can assist in identifying individuals who may be at risk for specific disorders by examining their medical history and the symptoms listed in electronic health records.

Additionally, NLP is essential to the creation of educational resources. Intelligent tutoring systems leverage natural language processing (NLP) to deliver individualized learning experiences by interpreting student responses and producing pertinent feedback. Moreover, automatic essay scoring systems that assess and score student essays based on substance, coherence, and language use employ natural language processing (NLP). By offering individualized learning routes and immediate feedback, these apps improve the quality of the educational experience's quality.

Sophisticated models and algorithms have been the driving force behind NLP breakthroughs. Handcrafted features and rule-based techniques were significant components of early NLP systems. However, deep learning and machine learning development have entirely changed the industry. Word embeddings, which encode words as high-dimensional vectors capturing their semantic meaning, were first introduced by models such as Word2Vec and GloVe. By giving words and their relationships better representations, these embeddings enhanced the performance of NLP systems.

NLP has expanded even further with the advent of transformer-based models like T5 (Text-to-Text Transfer Transformer), GPT (Generative Pre-trained Transformer), and BERT (Bidirectional Encoder Representations from Transformers). These models achieve state-of-the-art performance across several benchmarks because they have been pre-trained on large corpora of text data and fine-tuned on specific tasks. For example, BERT can better comprehend the subtleties of language since it can record the context of words in a sentence in both directions. GPT has demonstrated remarkable performance in tasks such as text completion, summarization, and translation, owing to its capacity to produce cohesive and contextually appropriate text.

Even with all of the advancements, NLP still needs help. It still needs to be easier for machines to understand sarcasm, idioms, context, and unclear language. Ethical issues such as privacy problems and bias in language models must also be considered to guarantee the appropriate use of NLP technology.

In summary, the dynamic and quickly developing field of natural language processing makes it possible for computers to comprehend and communicate with human language. Its uses have significantly impacted several sectors, from chatbots and sentiment analysis to machine translation and search engines. NLP has reached new heights thanks to deep learning and machine learning developments, which have made it possible to interpret language more accurately and sophisticatedly. NLP has enormous potential to transform communication and technology as long as research is focused on addressing current issues.

Text preprocessing and feature extraction

Fundamental Natural Language Processing (NLP) processes include text preprocessing and feature extraction. These procedures convert unstructured textual input into a format that can be analyzed and interpreted by machine learning algorithms. Building reliable NLP models that perform highly accurate and efficient tasks like sentiment analysis, text classification, and information retrieval requires compelling text preprocessing and feature extraction.

Several procedures are used in text preprocessing to standardize and clean the unprocessed text data. Text normalization is typically the initial stage, transforming the text into a consistent format. To maintain consistency, all characters should be lowercase. Punctuation that does not add to the meaning should also be removed, as should any unnecessary whitespace. Normalization guarantees that words are handled consistently by the model and contributes to the text's reduction in complexity.

Tokenization is an additional crucial stage of preprocessing. It entails dividing the text into smaller chunks known as tokens, which can be letters, words, or subwords. It is essential because tokenization enables the model to handle distinct textual components rather than considering the entire text as a single string. Tokenization would separate the line "The quick brown fox jumps over the lazy dog" into individual words or tokens. Several tokenization strategies include sub word tokenization, which breaks words into more manageable, meaningful pieces, and word tokenization, which splits text into spaces.

Stop word removal is a popular preprocessing technique in which frequently used words with little, or no meaning are eliminated from the text. Stuff like "the," "is," "in," and "and" are regarded as stop words because they are commonly used but don't offer helpful information for the majority of NLP jobs. Eliminating stop words concentrates the model's attention on the text's more informative passages while lowering data noise.

Lemmatization and stemming are methods for breaking words down to their most basic or root form. In the stemming process, words are trimmed to their stem, which isn't necessarily a legitimate word. One might reduce terms like "running," "runner," and "ran" to just "run." Conversely, lemmatization returns words to their dictionary or base form, which is always valid. As an illustration, "better" would lemmatize to "good." These methods aid in lowering the text's dimensionality and guarantee that many word forms are interpreted as a single characteristic.

The process of turning the preprocessed text into numerical representations that machine learning algorithms can comprehend is known as feature extraction. The Bag of Words (BoW) concept is a widely utilized and straightforward method. Using this method, the text is shown as a vector of word counts, with each dimension denoting a distinct word from the corpus and the value indicating the word's frequency in the document. BoW is simple to use, but it has drawbacks, like not considering word context and order.

The Term Frequency-Inverse Document Frequency (TF-IDF) model was created to overcome these drawbacks. TF-IDF gives every word a weight based on its rarity in overall texts (inverse document frequency) and its frequency in a document (term frequency). This strategy minimizes standard terms in multiple documents while emphasizing significant words inside a particular document. Information retrieval and text categorization problems benefit significantly from the usage of TF-IDF.

Words are represented as dense vectors in a continuous vector space using word embeddings, a more sophisticated feature extraction method. By grouping related words closer together in the vector space, word embeddings capture the semantic meaning of words, in contrast to BoW and TF-IDF, which generate sparse and high-dimensional representations. A few well-liked word embedding models are GloVe, Word2Vec, and Fast Text. These models can be adjusted for particular tasks and are usually pre-trained on sizable corpora. Word embeddings have helped natural language processing (NLP) models perform much better by assisting them to understand the links between words better.

Words in context are represented by contextual word embeddings generated via transformer-based models such as BERT (Bidirectional Encoder Representations from Transformers) and GPT (Generative Pre-trained Transformer). Contextual embeddings provide distinct vectors for the same word depending on its context inside a sentence, unlike typical word embeddings that assign a single vector to each word. This enables the program to distinguish between words with numerous meanings and capture nuanced meanings. For instance, the meaning of the word "bank" would change if it were used to describe a riverbank as opposed to a financial organization.

Dimensionality reduction, which attempts to minimize the number of features while maintaining the most significant information, is another essential feature extraction component. Singular value decomposition (SVD) and principal component analysis (PCA) are two methods that can be used to reduce the dimensionality of word embeddings and other numerical representations. This expedites training and enhances model performance by eliminating redundant or poorly informative elements.

Another crucial step in the feature extraction process is feature engineering. New characteristics are extracted from the text data already in existence to improve the model's capacity for learning and prediction. For instance, sentiment analysis allows engineering factors to enhance the model's accuracy, such as the usage of expressive punctuation, the length of the text, or the presence of particular keywords.

The NLP pipeline's essential stages of text preparation and feature extraction convert unstructured textual data into meaningful and structured numerical representations. Normalization, tokenization, stop word elimination, stemming, and lemmatization are text preprocessing operations that tidy and standardize the text. TF-IDF, Bag of Words, word embeddings, contextual embeddings, and other feature extraction approaches transform the text into numerical forms interpreted by machine learning algorithms.

Sentiment analysis, text classification, and language modeling

Three crucial tasks in Natural Language Processing (NLP) with broad applicability across multiple fields are sentiment analysis, text categorization, and language modeling. Every task focuses on a different facet of comprehending and interpreting human language, allowing machines to extract valuable information from textual data and carry out intricate language-related tasks.

Opinion mining, or sentiment analysis, identifies a text's sentiment or emotional tone. Completing this activity is crucial to comprehending social media interactions, consumer feedback, and public opinion. Sentiment analysis may classify text as good, harmful, or neutral. In more advanced algorithms, it can even identify subtle emotions such as surprise, excitement, rage, or grief. Text preprocessing is the first step, during which the text is cleaned and tokenized. After that, features are extracted using techniques such as word embeddings, TF-IDF, and Bag of Words. The emotion of fresh, unseen text is subsequently classified using machine learning models trained on labeled datasets. These models include logistic regression, support vector machines, and neural networks.

Sentiment analysis has a wide range of uses. Businesses utilize sentiment analysis in marketing to determine how customers feel about goods and services, which enables them to make data-driven decisions that increase customer happiness. Sentiment analysis in politics aids in tracking public opinion toward political candidates and policy. Sentiment analysis is a tool social media companies use to identify and handle offensive or damaging content. Despite its wide range of applications, sentiment analysis has limitations in processing language specific to a given subject, detecting sarcasm, and recognizing context. Enhancements in deep learning, namely in applying transformer models such as BERT and GPT, have led to notable improvements in sentiment analysis systems' precision and resilience.

Text classification is an essential NLP activity that classifies text documents into predetermined groups. This task is necessary to manage and organize massive amounts of text data. Text categorization can be multi-class (e.g., classifying news articles into sports, politics, and technology categories) or binary (e.g., spam vs. non-spam). Text preprocessing and feature extraction are the first steps in text categorization. Other machine-learning methods can be used once the text has been converted to numerical representations. More sophisticated techniques employ transformers, recurrent neural networks (RNNs), convolutional neural networks (CNNs), and k-nearest neighbors in addition to traditional algorithms like Naive Bayes and decision trees.

There are many real-world uses for text classification. Text classification is used in email filtering to distinguish between authentic and spam communications. It aids in the classification and suggestion of pertinent articles, movies, or goods to consumers in content recommendation systems according to their interests. Text classification is essential to document management systems' ability to organize and retrieve data effectively. It helps with document and record sorting and categorization for more straightforward access and analysis in the legal and medical areas.

The third major challenge, language modeling, is comprehending and forecasting language structure and meaning. The objective of a language model is to produce or identify logical word sequences that accurately represent the statistical characteristics of a language. Applications for language models include speech recognition, machine translation, text production, and more. Conventional language models, such as n-grams, use the preceding n words to predict the probability of a given word.

Deep learning has created more potent language models, including transformers, LSTMs (Long Short-Term Memory Networks), and RNNs. Because RNNs and LSTMs can handle sequential data and record dependencies across time steps, language modeling jobs can benefit from their use. They still have issues with training efficiency and long-term dependence, though. Transformers have revolutionized language modeling by leveraging self-attention processes to record correlations between all words in a sequence at once. Transformers were first introduced with the "Attention is All You Need" article. As a result, highly successful models like BERT, GPT, and T5 have been developed.

Bidirectional Encoder Representations from Transformers, or BERT, is a pre-trained model that can comprehend the context in both directions, which improves its ability to interpret word meanings. With its fine-tuning for various NLP tasks, BERT achieves cutting-edge outcomes in question answering, text classification, and other areas. Based on prompts, GPT (Generative Pre-trained Transformer), in particular GPT-3, has shown impressive text creation skills, generating coherent and contextually appropriate content.

Language modeling has a wide range of revolutionary applications. Language models translate text between languages; models such as Google's Neural Machine Translation (GNMT) produce accurate translations. Language models give chatbots and virtual assistants the conversational AI capability to converse naturally and meaningfully with users. Applications for text generation include content creation, where models can write short stories, articles, or even bits of code.

Despite noteworthy progress, language modeling faces obstacles like data bias, processing demands, and moral dilemmas. Pre-trained models might unwittingly learn and perpetuate biases in the training data, leading to unfair or detrimental outcomes. These models need a lot of processing power to train on a big scale, which raises accessibility and environmental issues. One ethical concern is the possible abuse of text creation tools to produce damaging or deceptive information.

In conclusion, sentiment analysis, text classification, and language modeling are basic tasks in NLP that enable machines to understand and interact with human language efficiently. These tasks use various methods and models, ranging from sophisticated deep learning frameworks like transformers to conventional machine learning algorithms. Their applications cover several fields, from marketing and politics to healthcare and education, proving the revolutionary impact of NLP on technology and society. There is still much room for creativity and advancement in language-related jobs as long as a study of the difficulties and limits of natural language processing (NLP) persists.

Advanced topics: Transformers, BERT, GPT models

Transformers, BERT, and GPT models represent some of the most advanced topics in natural language processing (NLP). These architectures have revolutionized how machines understand and generate human language, enabling various applications from machine translation to conversational agents.

The transformer model, introduced in the seminal paper "Attention is All You Need" by Vaswani et al. in 2017, marked a significant departure from the traditional sequence-to-sequence models that relied heavily on recurrent neural networks (RNNs) and their variants like LSTMs (Long Short-Term Memory networks). The primary innovation of the transformer architecture is the self-attention mechanism, which allows the model to weigh the importance of different words in a sentence when encoding a particular word.

Transformers consist of an encoder-decoder structure where the encoder processes the input sequence, and the decoder generates the output sequence. However, many subsequent models have employed the encoder or the decoder, depending on the specific task. The self-attention mechanism is complemented by positional encodings, which help the model understand the order of words in a sequence, as transformers lack the inherent sequential structure of RNNs.

Devlin et al. introduced the Bidirectional Encoder Representations from Transformers (BERT) model on the foundation of transformers in 2018. BERT is designed to pre-train deep bidirectional representations by joint conditioning on the left and right context in all layers. This bi-directionality allows BERT to understand the context of a word based on its surrounding words more comprehensively. BERT is pre-trained on a large corpus using two tasks: masked language modeling (MLM) and next sentence prediction (NSP). In MLM, some percentage of the input tokens are masked randomly, and the model learns to predict them based on their context.

BERT's pre-training approach enables it to capture nuanced linguistic information and perform well across various NLP tasks after fine-tuning specific datasets. Its release set new NLP benchmarks, including the General Language Understanding Evaluation (GLUE) and the Stanford Question Answering Dataset (SQuAD).

Generative Pre-trained Transformers (GPT) take another approach to utilizing transformer architecture, emphasizing language generation. The first GPT model was introduced by OpenAI in 2018, followed by GPT-2 in 2019, and the even more advanced GPT-3 in 2020. Unlike BERT, which uses a bidirectional approach, GPT models are based on a unidirectional transformer architecture, meaning they generate text one word at a time, considering the previous words in the sequence.

GPT models are pre-trained on vast amounts of text data using a simple yet effective objective: predicting the next word in a sequence. This autoregressive training allows GPT models to generate coherent and contextually relevant text, making them highly effective for tasks like text completion, translation, summarization, and even creative writing. GPT-3, the series's largest and most powerful version at its release, contains 175 billion parameters, making it capable of understanding and generating human-like text with remarkable fluency and coherence.

One of the critical strengths of GPT-3 is its ability to perform tasks with few-shot, one-shot, or even zero-shot learning. With little to no task-specific training data, GPT-3 can still provide impressive performance based on the general knowledge it acquired during pre-training. This capability has opened up new possibilities for applications where obtaining large, annotated datasets is challenging.

Despite their success, these models have limitations. BERT and GPT models require significant computational resources for training and fine-tuning, making them inaccessible for smaller organizations or individuals without substantial hardware capabilities. Additionally, their large size and complexity can lead to issues with interpretability, as understanding why a model makes a particular prediction can be challenging.

In conclusion, transformers, BERT, and GPT models have profoundly impacted the field of NLP, pushing the boundaries of what machines can achieve in understanding and generating human language. Their innovations in self-attention mechanisms, bidirectional context understanding, and autoregressive text generation have set new standards for performance and versatility in NLP tasks. As research continues and these models evolve, they promise even more incredible advancements, bringing us closer to the goal of seamless human-machine interaction and understanding.

CHAPTER VII

Computer Vision

Introduction to computer vision

Within artificial intelligence (AI), computer vision is a fast-developing discipline that allows machines to analyze and make judgments based on visual data. This multidisciplinary field integrates concepts from mathematics, computer science, engineering, and neurology to create systems that can see, comprehend, and interact with images in a way comparable to human vision.

Computer vision began when scientists started experimenting with how machines could interpret visual data in the 1960s and 1970s. Early efforts used primitive methods and little computing power, concentrating on straightforward tasks like shape recognition and edge detection.

The introduction of machine learning, particularly the creation of convolutional neural networks (CNNs), was a significant advance in computer vision. CNN changed the field by offering a potent feature extraction and pattern identification tool. The composition and operation of the human visual cortex inspired them. Because of its hierarchical structure, CNNs are well-suited for tasks like object detection, segmentation, and picture classification. They can also automatically learn and recognize features from raw pixel data.

In computer vision, one of the most essential jobs is image classification. It entails classifying or labeling an input image according to its visual content. In several benchmark datasets, CNNs have outperformed humans in this domain, demonstrating extraordinary accomplishment. Large-scale annotated datasets like ImageNet, which have millions of classified photos covering hundreds of categories, have made this possible. These datasets give CNNs the training data they need to understand and extrapolate from various visual patterns.

Object detection expands the capabilities of image classification by locating items in an image using bounding boxes and determining their presence. This task is more complicated because the model must account for changes in object scale, orientation, and occlusion. To overcome these difficulties, methods like SSD (Single Shot MultiBox Detector), YOLO (You Only Look Once), and Region-based CNNs (R-CNN) have been created. These methods allow real-time object recognition applications in robotics, autonomous driving, and surveillance.

Image segmentation, which divides an image into meaningful sections corresponding to various objects or structures, is another crucial task in computer vision. A thorough comprehension of the scene is produced by giving each pixel in the image a class name using semantic segmentation. One step further is instance segmentation, which distinguishes between different instances of the same object category. Approaches like Mask R-CNN and Fully Convolutional Networks (FCNs) have made significant progress toward obtaining high efficiency and accuracy in segmentation tasks.

Computer vision includes various applications and research fields beyond these fundamental functions. Facial recognition is one well-known application widely used in social networking, security, and authentication. Computer vision systems can identify people with high accuracy by examining face traits and patterns, but this technology also has privacy and ethical issues.

There is also ongoing research in medical imaging, where computer vision algorithms can diagnose illnesses and ailments from medical scans, including X-rays, MRIs, and

CT scans. Automated medical image analysis can be used to identify abnormalities, monitor the course of diseases, and assist medical professionals in making decisions. This might lessen the workload for medical personnel and greatly enhance healthcare outcomes.

In addition, computer vision is essential to the advancement of driverless cars. For safe navigation, self-driving cars use a variety of sensors, including cameras, LIDAR, and other sensors. To detect and track objects, identify traffic signs, and comprehend road conditions, computer vision algorithms interpret the visual input. This allows the car to make decisions about its course in real-time.

Computer vision still faces several difficulties despite its impressive advancements. Achieving robustness and generalization in various uncertain contexts is one of the main challenges. How objects appear, the lighting, and the weather significantly impact how well vision systems work. Furthermore, a significant obstacle to training is still the necessity for a lot of labeled data, which has led to research on unsupervised and semi-supervised learning strategies.

Furthermore, it is impossible to ignore the ethical concerns of computer vision technology. Regulation and careful thought must be given to monitoring, privacy, and bias in facial recognition and other uses. To be responsibly deployed in society, computer vision systems must be fair, transparent, and accountable.

In summary, computer vision aims to mimic and improve human visual abilities. It is a dynamic and transformational discipline. Computer vision has come a long way from its early days to the state-of-the-art methods used today, making it possible for machines to comprehend and interact with the visual environment. With further advancements in science and technology, computer vision holds immense promise for revolutionizing businesses and enhancing lives worldwide.

Image preprocessing and augmentation

Within artificial intelligence (AI), computer vision is a fast-developing discipline that allows machines to analyze and make judgments based on visual data. This multidisciplinary field integrates concepts from mathematics, computer science, engineering, and neurology to create systems that can see, comprehend, and interact with images in a way comparable to human vision. Automating activities that the human visual system can perform, such as object and scene recognition and action and interaction interpretation, is the main objective of computer vision.

Computer vision began when scientists started experimenting with how machines could interpret visual data in the 1960s and 1970s. Early efforts used essential phases in the pipeline for computer vision and machine learning tasks, including image preprocessing and augmentation. By improving image quality and diversifying training data, these procedures produce more reliable and accurate models. While augmentation creates an artificial training dataset to increase the model's generalization capacity, picture preparation converts unprocessed image data into a format appropriate for analysis.

The first step in ensuring consistency and quality is image preprocessing, where raw picture data is cleaned and normalized. Resizing is a popular preprocessing method that evens out image dimensions. Neural networks usually require fixed-size inputs; therefore, this is crucial. For example, models such as convolutional neural networks (CNNs) typically require images to have a particular dimension, like 224x224 pixels.

Another critical stage in preprocessing is normalization. It entails converting an image's pixel values to a standard scale, typically between 0 and 1 or -1 and 1. This standardization aids in both speeding up and stabilizing neural network training. Normalization ensures that the distribution of the input data is consistent, which keeps any one feature from unduly affecting the model's predictions.

Denoising images is another crucial preprocessing method. Noise is frequently present in real-world images because of various issues, such as imperfect sensors or dim illumination. The underlying objects are represented more accurately and clearly when this undesired noise is reduced through denoising methods like median or Gaussian filters. Consequently, this improves computer vision models' performance.

Contrast correction is another preprocessing technique used to enhance an image's visual quality. It entails emphasizing the contrasts between an image's bright and dark regions. Improved contrast can be achieved using methods like histogram equalization or contrast-limited adaptive histogram equalization (CLAHE), which facilitates model feature detection and recognition.

Augmentation solves the problem of insufficient training data while preprocessing guarantees the consistency and quality of picture data. By applying numerous changes to the original photos, image augmentation artificially enhances the amount and diversity of the training dataset. Exposing models to a greater variety of variances during training aids in their improved generalization to new, unexplored data.

The rotation of photographs by a specific angle is a popular enhancement technique. This aids in making the model object orientation invariant. For example, there might be significant variations in the orientation of objects when performing tasks like object detection or recognition. The model gains the ability to recognize objects in any orientation using rotation-based training on photographs.

The technique of flipping, which involves both horizontal and vertical flips, is another popular augmentation technique. When it comes to tasks like facial recognition or generic object detection, horizontal flipping works incredibly well when an object's left- or right-oriented orientation has no bearing on its recognition. Although less prevalent, vertical flipping has specific uses, such as the study of aerial photography.

Scaling and cropping are other augmentation techniques that change the viewpoint and scale of photographs. To simulate items appearing at varying distances from the camera, scaling entails resizing images by various factors. Contrarily, cropping entails choosing arbitrary portions of an image. Concentrating the model's attention on distinct regions of the image helps improve the model's capacity to identify and detect objects in various situations.

Another effective technique for altering an image's color is color augmentation. Adjusting brightness, contrast, saturation, and hue are some techniques that create different lighting and color schemes. Because of this, the model is more resilient to variations in color and lighting, which are frequent in real-world situations.

Using geometric modifications such as perspective warping, applying blurring effects, and adding noise are examples of advanced augmentation techniques. Adding noise can assist the model in learning to deal with noisy inputs by simulating defects found in the actual world. Blurring can imitate out-of-focus photos to teach the model to detect objects even when they are not perfectly crisp. The training data is further diversified by geometric manipulations such as perspective warping, which alters the spatial relationships within the image.

Generative adversarial networks (GANs) are a prominent augmentation technique that produces lifelike synthetic visuals. A generator and a discriminator, two neural networks competing to create and assess artificial images, make up a GAN. When collecting genuine photos is difficult or costly, this technique can produce high-quality, diversified images that significantly improve the training dataset.

In conclusion, image preprocessing and augmentation methods are essential to studying computer vision and machine learning. Model training is made more accessible by preprocessing, which guarantees consistent, high-quality images. Conversely, augmentation introduces diversity into the training dataset by artificially growing it, improving the models' capacity to generalize to new data. Combined, these procedures are essential for creating reliable and accurate computer vision systems that function well in various settings and applications. Primitive methods and little computing power concentrate on straightforward tasks like shape recognition and edge detection. These early research projects established the foundation for more advanced methods appearing in the following decades.

The introduction of machine learning, particularly the creation of convolutional neural networks (CNNs), was a significant advance in computer vision. CNN changed the field by offering a potent feature extraction and pattern identification tool. The composition and operation of the human visual cortex inspired them. Because of its hierarchical structure, CNNs are well-suited for tasks like object detection, segmentation, and picture classification. They can also automatically learn and recognize features from raw pixel data.

In computer vision, one of the most essential jobs is image classification. It entails classifying or labeling an input image according to its visual content. In several benchmark datasets, CNNs have outperformed humans in this domain, demonstrating extraordinary accomplishment. Large-scale annotated datasets like ImageNet, which have millions of classified photos covering hundreds of categories, have made this possible.

Object detection expands the capabilities of image classification by locating items in an image using bounding boxes and determining their presence. This task is more complicated because the model must account for changes in object scale, orientation, and occlusion. To overcome these difficulties, methods like SSD (Single Shot MultiBox Detector), YOLO (You Only Look Once), and Region-based CNNs (R-CNN) have been created.

Image segmentation, which divides an image into meaningful sections corresponding to various objects or structures, is another crucial task in computer vision. A thorough comprehension of the scene is produced by giving each pixel in the image a class name using semantic segmentation. One step further is instance segmentation, which distinguishes between different instances of the same object category. Approaches like Mask R-CNN and Fully Convolutional Networks (FCNs) have made significant progress toward obtaining high efficiency and accuracy in segmentation tasks.

Computer vision includes various applications and research fields beyond these fundamental functions. Facial recognition is one well-known application widely used in social networking, security, and authentication. Computer vision systems can identify people with high accuracy by examining face traits and patterns, but this technology also has privacy and ethical issues.

There is also ongoing research in medical imaging, where computer vision algorithms can diagnose illnesses and ailments from medical scans, including X-rays, MRIs, and CT scans. Automated medical image analysis can be used to identify abnormalities, monitor the course of diseases, and assist medical professionals in making decisions. This might lessen the workload for medical personnel and greatly enhance healthcare outcomes.

In addition, computer vision is essential to the advancement of driverless cars. For safe navigation, self-driving cars use a variety of sensors, including cameras, LIDAR, and other sensors. To detect and track objects, identify traffic signs, and comprehend road conditions, computer vision algorithms interpret the visual input. This allows the car to make decisions about its course in real-time.

Computer vision still faces several difficulties despite its impressive advancements. Achieving robustness and generalization in various uncertain contexts is one of the main challenges. How objects appear, the lighting, and the weather significantly impact how well vision systems work. Furthermore, a significant obstacle to training is still the necessity for a lot of labeled data, which has led to research on unsupervised and semi-supervised learning strategies.

Furthermore, it is impossible to ignore the ethical concerns of computer vision technology. Regulation and careful thought must be given to monitoring, privacy, and bias in facial recognition and other uses. To be responsibly deployed in society, computer vision systems must be fair, transparent, and accountable.

In summary, computer vision aims to mimic and improve human visual abilities. It is a dynamic and transformational discipline. Computer vision has come a long way from its early days to the state-of-the-art methods used today, making it possible for machines to comprehend and interact with the visual environment. With further advancements in science and technology, computer vision holds immense promise for revolutionizing businesses and enhancing lives worldwide.

Object detection, image classification, and segmentation

In the science of computer vision, object recognition, picture classification, and segmentation are three essential activities that each have a unique function in helping machines comprehend and interpret visual input.

The process of giving a whole image a label based on its content is known as image classification. It is the most fundamental type of visual recognition and the basis for more intricate computer vision applications. Image classification aims to find the main subject or items in a picture and classify them into predetermined groups. To train a model to identify patterns and features associated with each class, a sizable dataset of annotated images is used. Because Convolutional Neural Networks (CNNs) can automatically build hierarchical feature representations from raw pixel data, they are the most often used models for image categorization.

By localizing objects with bounding boxes and detecting their presence in an image, object detection enhances the possibilities of image classification. This means that in addition to identifying the objects' presence, object detection models must also identify their locations within the image. Object recognition is a more challenging operation because the model must handle object size, orientation, and occlusion fluctuations. To overcome these difficulties, methods like SSD (Single Shot MultiBox Detector), YOLO (You Only Look Once), and Region-based CNNs (R-CNN) have been developed. One of the first models to use a two-stage method for object detection—generating region recommendations first, then categorizing them—was R-CNN, which Ross Girshick introduced in 2014. YOLO, first presented by Joseph Redmon et al., adopts a different strategy: treating object detection as a single regression issue and using entire images to forecast bounding boxes and class probabilities in a single evaluation. Because of this, YOLO is now faster and more appropriate for real-time applications. Wei Liu et al.'s SSD technology blends the concepts of old-fashioned detection techniques and YOLO by predicting item locations and categories using a single deep neural network, thus striking a solid balance between speed and accuracy.

Segmentation provides a pixel-by-pixel comprehension of the image, which advances object detection. Object segmentation divides a picture into meaningful sections corresponding to distinct items or structures, whereas object detection uses bounding boxes to identify and localize objects. Semantic and instance segmentation are the two primary categories of segmentation. Semantic segmentation divides the image into sections representing several item categories by giving a class label to every pixel in the picture. For this purpose, the model must have a fine-grained understanding of object boundaries and context. One of the first models to show the value of deep learning for semantic segmentation was the Fully Convolutional Network (FCN), developed by Jonathan Long et al. by substituting convolutional layers for the fully connected layers of conventional CNNs, enabling the network to produce dense predictions for every pixel. The encoder-decoder design of U-Net, a model created for biomedical image segmentation, has also helped it gain popularity by allowing for precise localization and capturing context at many scales.

Semantic segmentation differs from instance segmentation, which differentiates between various instances of an object category. This implies that every example of an item is given a distinct label, enabling the model to distinguish between different objects even when they are members of the same class. Mask R-CNN is a popular model, for instance, segmentation, that expands the Faster R-CNN object detection framework. Mask R-CNN, first presented by Kaiming He et al., allows the model to produce high-quality masks for every object it detects by adding a branch for segmentation mask prediction with the branches already in place for classification and bounding box regression.

Image classification, object identification, and segmentation are three related tasks frequently combined in different applications. For instance, segmentation can be used in autonomous driving to define lanes and limits on the road, object detection can be used to find other cars and pedestrians, and picture classification can be used to identify traffic signs and lights. These tasks, which involve identifying various cell types, detecting malignancies, and segmenting anatomical regions, can aid in diagnosing diseases in medical imaging.

Despite the noteworthy advancements in the past few years, obstacles are still to be overcome to achieve robustness and generalization in various intricate real-world circumstances. Occlusions, background clutter, and lighting variations can all impact how well computer vision models operate. Additionally, a significant bottleneck in training is the requirement for sizable, annotated datasets, which has prompted research into semi-supervised and unsupervised learning methods.

To sum up, computer vision tasks such as object identification, image classification, and segmentation are critical to the ability of machines to perceive and process visual data. These domains have significantly improved due to profound learning breakthroughs, with models exhibiting astounding accuracy and efficiency. As research into them advances, these activities will be essential in developing intelligent systems that can perform a wide range of jobs, from medical diagnostics to autonomous vehicles.

Advanced techniques: Generative Adversarial Networks (GANs) and Style Transfer

Advanced methods in artificial intelligence and computer vision, such as Generative Adversarial Networks (GANs) and Style Transfer, have drawn much interest for their capacity to create and modify images in fresh and visually appealing ways. These deep learning-based methods have created new opportunities for innovation, data augmentation, and valuable applications across various sectors.

In 2014, Ian Goodfellow and associates introduced Generative Adversarial Networks (GANs), a revolutionary method for generative modeling. A generator and a discriminator neural network, trained concurrently in a competitive context, make up a GAN. The discriminator's job is to discern between actual and fake data, whereas the generator produces convincing synthetic data, like images, from random noise. The discriminator wants to get better at spotting fakes, and the generator intends to provide data that can trick the discriminator.

The success of one network depends on the failure of the other in a zero-sum game that forms the basis of GAN design. As training continues, the discriminator improves at picking up on minute flaws while the generator produces realistic images. This dynamic interaction results in the constant improvement of both networks, delivering high-quality synthetic images. GANs have been effectively used for many tasks, such as creating realistic human faces, super-resolution, inpainting, and image synthesis.

Creating conditional GANs (cGANs), in which data generation is conditioned on particular input factors, is one of the fantastic developments in GANs. More control over the created photos is made possible by this. cGANs, for instance, can produce images from text descriptions, making it possible to create highly detailed and contextually appropriate images from straightforward text prompts. The development of Progressive GANs, which produce high-resolution images by gradually increasing the resolution from low-resolution training sets, is another noteworthy breakthrough.

Another sophisticated technique is "style transfer," which modifies an image's look without changing its substance. The use of convolutional neural networks (CNNs) to separate and recombine the content and style of images was made famous by Leon Gatys, Alexander Ecker, and Matthias Bethge in 2015. The basic concept of style transfer is to combine two images, a content image, and a style image, so that the final image keeps the content image's identifiable content while including the style image's distinctive components.

To achieve style transfer, an image must be optimized to reduce the contrast between its style features and those of the style image and the difference between its content features and those of the image. Higher layers of a pre-trained CNN, which reflect the high-level structure and objects in the image, are usually where content features are recorded.

In artistic applications, style transfer has been widely employed to create visuals that combine photographs and the styles of well-known artists, such as Van Gogh or Picasso. This method can also change entire video sequences to a particular artistic style in video processing. Additionally, the fashion and design sectors have investigated style transfer, which enables designers to play around with various textures and patterns in their works.

GANs and Style Transfer mainly rely on deep learning methods, especially convolutional neural networks to get such remarkable outcomes. These techniques have significantly increased the range of imaginative and practical AI applications. GANs have pushed the limits of human creativity in entertainment and art by creating original songs, artwork, and even movie scripts.

Even with their achievements, GANs and Style Transfer still need to improve. Due to issues including mode collapse, in which the generator generates a finite number of different types of input, and instability during the adversarial training phase, GAN training is infamously challenging. While spectral normalization and Wasserstein GANs (WGANs) are two methods researchers have devised to stabilize GAN training, these are still active research areas.

In conclusion, two of the most fascinating developments in artificial intelligence and computer vision are Generative Adversarial Networks and Style Transfer. The production of incredibly realistic synthetic data with a wide range of applications in entertainment and the arts has been made possible by GANs, which have completely transformed the area of generative modeling.

CHAPTER VIII

AI in the Cloud

Benefits of cloud-based AI solutions

Cloud-based AI solutions offer numerous benefits, transforming how businesses and organizations deploy and manage artificial intelligence technologies. These advantages span scalability, cost efficiency, accessibility, collaboration, security, and the ability to leverage advanced tools and services.

One of the primary benefits of cloud-based AI solutions is scalability. Cloud platforms provide unlimited computing resources, enabling organizations to scale their AI applications up or down based on demand. This flexibility is crucial for handling large datasets and running complex machine-learning models requiring significant computational power. Unlike traditional on-premises infrastructure, which physical hardware constraints can limit, cloud-based solutions allow for dynamic resource allocation.

Cost efficiency is another significant advantage of cloud-based AI. Traditional AI infrastructure requires substantial upfront investment in servers, storage, and networking equipment, followed by ongoing maintenance and operational costs. Cloud services operate on a pay-as-you-go model, where organizations only pay for the resources they use. This model reduces the financial barrier to entry for AI adoption, making advanced technologies accessible to smaller businesses and startups.

Accessibility is a significant benefit of cloud-based AI solutions. These platforms provide access to powerful AI tools and frameworks over the Internet, enabling users to work from anywhere with an Internet connection. This democratizes access to advanced AI capabilities, allowing a more comprehensive range of users, including those in remote or underserved areas, to leverage AI for their needs.

Cloud-based AI solutions greatly enhance collaboration. These platforms facilitate seamless cooperation between teams, regardless of their geographical location. Multiple users can access, share, and work on the same AI models and datasets simultaneously, fostering a collaborative environment that enhances productivity and innovation. Cloud platforms also integrate with various tools and services that support version control, project management, and communication, making it easier for teams to coordinate their efforts and manage AI projects effectively.

Security is critical for organizations adopting AI technologies, and cloud-based solutions offer robust security features. Leading cloud providers invest heavily in security measures, including encryption, access controls, and regular security audits, to protect data and applications from threats. These providers comply with industry standards and regulations, ensuring that organizations can meet their compliance requirements.

Cloud-based AI solutions also provide access to cutting-edge tools and services. Major cloud providers, such as Amazon Web Services (AWS), Google Cloud Platform (GCP), and Microsoft Azure, offer a wide range of AI and machine learning services, including pre-trained models, automated machine learning (AutoML) tools, and custom model development environments.

The integration of cloud-based AI with other cloud services further enhances its capabilities. For example, AI solutions can be combined with extensive data analytics services to process and analyze large datasets in real time, providing valuable insights for decision-making.

Cloud platforms also offer seamless integration with Internet of Things (IoT) services, enabling the deployment of AI at the edge to process data from connected devices and make real-time decisions.

In addition to these benefits, cloud-based AI solutions promote innovation by providing a platform for experimentation and rapid prototyping. Organizations can quickly test new ideas and models without significant upfront investment. The flexibility and scalability of cloud platforms allow for iterative development, where models can be refined and improved based on feedback and new data.

Moreover, cloud-based AI solutions support continuous integration and continuous deployment (CI/CD) practices, ensuring that AI models are always up-to-date and performing optimally. Automated workflows can be set up to train, test, and deploy models, streamlining the development process and reducing the risk of errors. This automation enhances the reliability and performance of AI applications, making them more robust and scalable.

In conclusion, cloud-based AI solutions offer many benefits transforming organizations' development, deployment, and management of AI technologies. The scalability, cost efficiency, accessibility, collaboration, security, and access to advanced tools provided by cloud platforms make AI more accessible and practical for businesses of all sizes. These advantages not only lower the barrier to entry for AI adoption but also promote innovation and accelerate the development of AI-driven products and services. As cloud technology continues to evolve, the synergy between cloud computing and AI will drive further advancements, enabling organizations to harness the full potential of artificial intelligence.

Overview of cloud platforms: AWS, Azure, Google Cloud

Cloud platforms have become the backbone of modern computing, providing scalable, flexible, and cost-effective solutions for various applications. Among the leading providers of cloud services are Amazon Web Services (AWS), Microsoft Azure, and Google Cloud Platform (GCP). Each platform offers a comprehensive suite of services designed to meet the needs of businesses and developers. Still, they also have unique features and strengths that distinguish them from one another.

Amazon Web Services (AWS) is widely regarded as the cloud computing pioneer. Launched in 2006, AWS has become the world's most popular and extensively used cloud platform. It offers many services, including computing power, storage, databases, machine learning, analytics, networking, and more. One of the critical strengths of AWS is its extensive global infrastructure, which includes multiple regions and availability zones, ensuring high availability and redundancy.

The big 3 Cloud platforms

Microsoft Azure, launched in 2010, is a strong competitor in the cloud computing market, particularly in enterprise environments. Azure integrates seamlessly with

Microsoft's ecosystem of products, making it an attractive choice for organizations already using Microsoft technologies. Azure offers various services, including virtual machines, databases, AI and machine learning, IoT, and DevOps tools. One of the standout features of Azure is its hybrid cloud capabilities, which allow businesses to integrate their on-premises infrastructure with the cloud.

Google Cloud Platform (GCP) is known for its data analytics, machine learning, and container orchestration strengths. Launched in 2008, GCP leverages Google's expertise in infrastructure, artificial intelligence, and open-source technologies. GCP offers a comprehensive suite of services, including computing, storage, databases, big data analytics, machine learning, and networking.

Each cloud platform has its ecosystem of tools and services catering to different needs and use cases. With its extensive service portfolio and mature infrastructure, AWS is often the go-to choice for large enterprises and startups looking for a reliable and scalable cloud solution. AWS's pay-as-you-go pricing model and wide range of service tiers make it accessible to businesses of all sizes. Its strong focus on innovation, with frequent updates and new service launches, ensures customers access to the latest technologies.

With its strong integration with Microsoft's suite of products, Azure is a natural fit for businesses that rely on Windows Server, Active Directory, SQL Server, and other Microsoft technologies. Azure's hybrid cloud capabilities provide a seamless bridge between on-premises and cloud environments, making it an ideal choice for organizations with legacy infrastructure or specific regulatory requirements. Azure also offers comprehensive support for various development environments, including .NET, Java, Python, and Node.js, catering to a diverse developer community.

In conclusion, AWS, Azure, and Google Cloud Platform are the three leading cloud platforms, each offering a rich set of services and unique strengths that cater to different business needs and use cases. AWS is known for its extensive service portfolio and mature infrastructure, making it a reliable choice for enterprises and startups. Azure's seamless integration with Microsoft's ecosystem and hybrid cloud capabilities make it ideal for businesses already using Microsoft technologies. GCP's strengths in data analytics, machine learning, and container orchestration position it as a leader for organizations looking to leverage AI and modern cloud-native architectures.

Deploying AI models on the cloud

Deploying AI models on the cloud has become essential for modern organizations looking to leverage artificial intelligence for various applications. The cloud provides the infrastructure, scalability, and tools required to deploy, manage, and scale AI models efficiently. This approach simplifies the deployment process and ensures that AI models can operate at scale and integrate seamlessly with other services and applications.

The first step in deploying AI models on the cloud involves selecting an appropriate platform. Leading cloud service providers such as Amazon Web Services (AWS), Microsoft Azure, and Google Cloud Platform (GCP) offer various AI and machine learning services tailored to different needs. AWS provides services like Amazon SageMaker, which simplifies the process of building, training, and deploying machine learning models at scale. Azure offers Azure Machine Learning, a comprehensive suite of tools for managing the entire machine learning lifecycle.

Once the platform is selected, the next phase involves preparing the model for deployment. This preparation includes training the model, optimizing it for performance, and ensuring it meets the necessary accuracy and reliability standards. Training typically involves using large datasets to teach the model to perform specific tasks, such as image recognition, natural language processing, or predictive analytics. Cloud platforms provide powerful computational resources, such as GPUs and TPUs, significantly accelerating the training process.

After training, the model needs to be packaged and prepared for deployment. This involves converting the model into a format easily deployed on the cloud. Standard formats include TensorFlow SavedModel, ONNX (Open Neural Network Exchange), and PyTorch models. Packaging the model ensures it can seamlessly integrate with cloud services and other applications. Cloud platforms provide various tools and frameworks to simplify this process.

Deploying the model on the cloud involves several steps, starting with setting up the necessary infrastructure. Cloud platforms provide managed services for deploying models, which handle the underlying infrastructure, such as servers, storage, and networking. These services ensure the deployed models' high availability, scalability, and reliability.

One of the key advantages of deploying AI models on the cloud is the ability to scale. Cloud platforms provide auto-scaling capabilities that automatically adjust the computational resources based on the load and demand. This ensures that the AI models can handle varying traffic and workloads without manual intervention. For instance, during peak times, the cloud platform can allocate more resources to handle the increased demand, and during off-peak times, it can scale down to save costs.

Monitoring and management are another critical aspect of deploying AI models on the cloud. Once the model is deployed, monitoring its performance, usage, and health is essential. Cloud platforms provide comprehensive monitoring and logging tools that offer insights into model performance, latency, and error rates. These tools help organizations promptly identify and address issues, ensuring the models operate smoothly.

Security is a paramount concern when deploying AI models on the cloud. Cloud platforms offer robust security features to protect models and data. These features include encryption, access controls, and industry standards and regulations compliance. For instance, AWS provides AWS Identity and Access Management (IAM) to control access to resources and encryption services to protect data in transit and at rest.

In addition to deployment, maintaining and updating AI models is an ongoing process. Models must be retrained and updated regularly to adapt to new data and changing conditions. Cloud platforms provide tools for continuous integration and deployment (CI/CD) of AI models, enabling organizations to automate the retraining and deployment process.

In conclusion, deploying AI models on the cloud offers numerous benefits, including scalability, cost efficiency, accessibility, and robust security. Cloud platforms such as AWS, Azure, and GCP provide comprehensive tools and services that simplify AI model deployment, management, and scaling. By leveraging the cloud, organizations can focus on developing and optimizing their AI models while the cloud provider handles the underlying infrastructure and operational complexities.

Case studies of cloud-based AI implementations

Cloud-based AI applications are becoming increasingly common across various industries, providing solid answers to challenging issues and spurring creativity. Numerous case studies demonstrate how businesses have effectively used AI in the cloud to improve customer experiences, streamline processes, and gain a competitive edge.

One prominent example is Netflix, a streaming media leader whose recommendation engine is powered by Amazon Web Services (AWS). To tailor its users' viewing experiences, Netflix's recommendation engine, which powers more than 80% of the content streamed on the network, extensively uses machine learning techniques. Netflix takes advantage of massive computer resources and cutting-edge machine learning tools by implementing its AI models on AWS.

Another noteworthy example is the Royal Bank of Scotland (RBS), which used Microsoft Azure to build Cora, an AI-powered chatbot, to improve its customer service skills. RBS had to deal with many consumer requests, frequently resulting in lengthy wait times and higher operating expenses. RBS created Cora to help consumers with routine banking inquiries like account balances, transactions, and product information by utilizing Azure's AI services.

Google Cloud Platform (GCP) is used by Mount Sinai Health System in New York City in the healthcare industry to enhance patient outcomes via predictive analytics. Mount Sinai worked to create a predictive algorithm that would be able to identify people who might otherwise die from sepsis. Mount Sinai examined enormous volumes of patient data, including test results, vital signs, and electronic health records, using GCP's AI and machine learning capabilities.

Predictive maintenance is another way that General Electric (GE) uses AWS to enhance its industrial processes. Thousands of industrial machines and sensors provide data for GE's Predix Industrial Internet platform, which uses AWS's cloud infrastructure for data collection and analysis. GE can anticipate equipment breakdowns and minimize downtime by implementing machine learning models on AWS.

Sephora, a well-known international cosmetics shop, has improved its online and in-store consumer experience by utilizing cloud-based artificial intelligence (AI) via Microsoft Azure. Sephora has integrated an artificial intelligence (AI) virtual artist tool that allows consumers to test makeup using augmented reality (AR) virtually. Sephora's virtual artist uses Azure's machine learning and computer vision capabilities to virtually apply makeup and evaluate facial traits, giving customers a realistic preview of the items.

The London Metropolitan Police, which used GCP to create an AI-driven crime prediction system, is another noteworthy case study. To tackle the problem of efficiently allocating few resources for crime prevention, the Metropolitan Police leveraged GCP's machine learning capabilities to examine past crime data and detect trends. The police can more effectively assign patrols and anticipate crime hotspots by implementing predictive models on GCP.

Precision agriculture solutions powered by AI have been developed by John Deere, a top agricultural machinery manufacturer, using AWS. John Deere's cloud-based platform gathers data from sensors and GPS units mounted on farming machinery. John Deere can send farmers information on crop health, soil conditions, and the best times to plant by implementing machine learning models on AWS. With the help of these insights, farmers can make data-driven decisions that will boost agricultural yields while using fewer resources.

These case studies demonstrate how cloud-based AI systems can revolutionize various sectors. Organizations can create and implement AI solutions that spur creativity, increase productivity, and improve customer experiences by utilizing the scalability, processing capacity, and cutting-edge technologies offered by cloud platforms like AWS, Azure, and GCP. Because of its adaptability, cloud-based AI can be used for various purposes, including precision farming, predictive maintenance, personalized suggestions, and customer support.

CHAPTER IX

Integrating AI into Business Solutions

Identifying AI opportunities in business

For companies in various industries, seeing chances to incorporate artificial intelligence (AI) into daily operations has become crucial. Artificial intelligence (AI) technologies offer transformative capabilities promoting efficiency, innovation, and competitive advantage. These technologies range from computer vision and robotic process automation to machine learning and natural language processing. Companies may create new growth potential, enhance consumer experiences, and improve decision-making processes by identifying and capitalizing on AI opportunities.

Increasing operational efficiency is one of the main areas where AI offers substantial potential. Automating repetitive jobs with AI can speed up customer service inquiries, data entry, and backend operations. Robotic process automation (RPA) powered by artificial intelligence (AI) can automate repetitive operations in supply chain management, finance, and human resources, freeing human resources for higher-value work.

Utilizing AI for forecasting and predictive analytics presents another exciting possibility. AI algorithms can analyze large amounts of historical and current data to find trends, patterns, and insights that human analysts might miss. Businesses can use this expertise to forecast demand, identify market trends, anticipate customer behavior, and manage risk more accurately. Retail companies, for instance, can leverage AI-powered analytics to adjust pricing and inventory strategies in response to changes in customer preferences and demand.

Another area that is prime for AI-driven innovation is customer experience. Artificial intelligence (AI) tools that help organizations better understand customer sentiment and preferences include natural language processing (NLP) and sentiment analysis. Artificial intelligence (AI)-powered chatbots and virtual assistants can offer individualized customer care, instantly answer questions, and aid clients with their purchase decisions.

AI offers chances for new services and product development as well. Businesses can find holes in the market and create creative solutions that address new demands by examining customer input, market trends, and competitor insights. Recommendation engines driven by AI can make recommendations for new features or improvements to existing services based on user behavior and preferences, encouraging innovation and ongoing improvement.

AI also presents chances to improve decision-making procedures via analytics and insights based on data. AI systems can analyze large, complicated datasets and give executives helpful information that helps them make strategic decisions. To help with product development, pricing strategies, and market expansion plans, AI-powered business intelligence solutions, for instance, may monitor sales trends, customer demographics, and market circumstances.

Another area where AI can significantly improve performance is supply chain management. AI-driven predictive analytics helps forecast demand, handle logistics more effectively, and optimize inventory levels. Artificial intelligence (AI)-enabled autonomous cars and drones can expedite delivery and warehouse operations, cutting costs and improving operational agility. AI-driven supply chain analytics may also help firms become more resilient and efficient by locating inefficiencies, bottlenecks, and cost-saving possibilities within the supply chain network.

Finally, AI offers chances to raise worker engagement and productivity at work. Artificial intelligence (AI)-powered applications and platforms can improve teamwork and communication, automate administrative duties, and offer individualized learning and development possibilities. AI-powered productivity tools and virtual assistants can improve business decision-making processes by facilitating information sharing, streamlining workflows, and streamlining workflows.

To sum up, recognizing AI potential in business necessitates using AI technology strategically to meet particular needs and seize new chances. Businesses may unleash AI's disruptive potential by concentrating on supply chain management, decision-making, customer experience, operational efficiency, predictive analytics, and workplace productivity. In addition to improving business performance, successfully implementing AI initiatives positions companies for long-term development, competitiveness, and innovation in an increasingly digital and data-driven environment

AI for decision making and automation

Artificial intelligence (AI) transforms automation and decision-making procedures in various industries by providing unseen capacities for data analysis, outcome prediction, and operational efficiency. AI-driven decision-making uses machine learning algorithms to evaluate large volumes of data and extract insightful information, improving efficiency, accuracy, and strategy alignment.

Predictive analytics is one of the main ways artificial intelligence is used in decision-making. AI systems can foresee future trends, consumer behavior, and market dynamics by analyzing historical and real-time data. Financial firms, for instance, utilize AI-powered predictive analytics to manage investment portfolios, detect fraud, and score credit. Artificial intelligence (AI) algorithms can detect suspicious activity or forecast market trends by evaluating transactional data and patterns.

AI is also essential for robotic process automation (RPA), which automates repetitive jobs and procedures. RPA mimics human behavior by using AI algorithms to automate repetitive operations like data input, processing invoices, and answering consumer inquiries. Organizations can lower manual error rates, expedite process execution, and reallocate human resources to more strategic endeavors by implementing RPA. For example, medical professionals can concentrate on patient care and essential decision-making using AI-powered RPA to automate administrative activities like patient scheduling and claims processing.

Furthermore, intelligent decision support systems that help managers and executives make well-informed judgments are a part of AI-driven automation. These systems use artificial intelligence (AI) methods, like machine learning models and natural language processing (NLP), to evaluate large, complicated datasets and produce insights that may be put to use. AI-driven business intelligence solutions, for instance, compile and examine market trends, sales data, and customer reviews to produce tailored suggestions and predictive analytics.

AI is revolutionizing clinical decision-making in the healthcare industry by offering individualized therapy recommendations and diagnostic assistance systems. AI algorithms examine genomic data, medical pictures, and patient records to help medical personnel diagnose illnesses, forecast outcomes, and suggest individualized treatment strategies. AI-powered diagnostic technologies, for example, have a high degree of accuracy when identifying anomalies in medical scans, which makes early identification and intervention easier.

Furthermore, AI-driven automation transforms supply chain management by streamlining transportation, demand forecasting, and inventory management. Supply chain data, such as supplier performance, inventory levels, and market demand, is analyzed by AI algorithms to forecast future needs and maximize resource allocation. Retail businesses, for instance, leverage supply chain analytics driven by AI to reduce carrying costs, increase delivery efficiency, and minimize stockouts.

Artificial intelligence (AI)-driven chatbots and virtual assistants are revolutionizing customer service and experience by offering individualized and effective customer support. These artificial intelligence (AI) systems use sentiment analysis and natural language understanding (NLU) to analyze client queries, deliver precise answers, and handle problems instantly. To increase customer pleasure and loyalty, e-commerce platforms, for instance, use AI chatbots to help with order tracking, troubleshooting, and product recommendations. Thanks to AI-driven customization algorithms, businesses can also offer customized recommendations and targeted marketing campaigns based on customer behavior and preferences.

Additionally, by tracking equipment performance and anticipating probable problems, artificial intelligence (AI) offers predictive maintenance in the manufacturing, energy, and transportation sectors. Artificial intelligence (AI) systems examine sensor data, operational metrics, and maintenance records to find abnormalities and trends suggestive of future issues. This proactive strategy lowers maintenance expenses, decreases unscheduled downtime, and increases asset longevity. For instance,

AI-driven predictive maintenance is used by industrial manufacturers to guarantee continuous operations, optimize production schedules, and enhance equipment durability.

In summary, artificial intelligence (AI) for automation and decision-making is a revolutionary force that boosts productivity, creativity, and industry competitiveness. Organizations can achieve operational excellence, enhance decision-making procedures, and provide outstanding customer experiences by utilizing AI-driven predictive analytics, robotic process automation, intelligent decision support systems, diagnostic tools, supply chain optimization, customer service automation, and predictive maintenance.

Building AI-driven applications

Using artificial intelligence (AI) technology to software solutions to improve functionality, automate processes, and offer intelligent insights is known as building AI-driven applications. Artificial intelligence (AI)-driven applications evaluate data, provide predictions, and adjust to changing circumstances by utilizing machine learning algorithms, natural language processing (NLP), computer vision, and other AI approaches. These applications are revolutionizing entire sectors by facilitating automation, enhancing decision-making procedures, and providing customized user experiences.

Preparing and preparing data is one of the core components of creating AI-driven apps. For AI models to learn and generalize, vast amounts of high-quality data are needed. Cleaning, converting, and organizing data to make sure it is correct, pertinent, and prepared for analysis is known as data preparation. This stage is essential for successfully training AI models and guaranteeing that they generate accurate results. For instance, to provide precise forecasts and suggestions for medical practitioners, AI-driven diagnostic systems in the healthcare industry rely on carefully selected datasets of patient records, medical pictures, and genomic data.

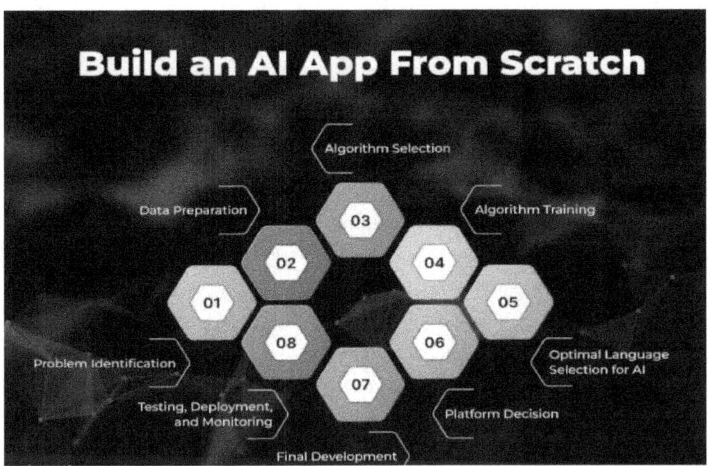

Many AI-driven applications are based on machine learning, which allows systems to learn from data and make predictions or judgments on their own. Supervised learning techniques like regression and classification are utilized for applications like image identification, speech recognition, and predictive analytics. Unsupervised learning methods, such as anomaly detection and clustering, can be used to extract insights and hidden patterns from data in the absence of labeled instances. Contrarily, reinforcement learning teaches AI systems through trial-and-error interactions with their surroundings, optimizing actions to meet predetermined objectives.

Another essential element of AI-driven applications is natural language processing (NLP), which enables machines to comprehend and produce human language. Thanks to NLP approaches, chatbots and virtual assistants can comprehend user inquiries, gather pertinent data, and make suitable responses in natural language. NLP applications that improve user-AI system engagement and communication include sentiment analysis, text summarization, and language translation. Customer service apps, for example, use natural language processing (NLP) to automate answers to consumer questions, increasing productivity and user happiness.

Another potent AI technique is computer vision, applied to tasks like deciphering and evaluating visual data from pictures or movies. Computer vision systems powered by AI can carry out tasks, including autonomous navigation, object identification, image classification, and facial recognition. These skills are helpful in fields like healthcare, where AI-driven diagnostic systems examine pictures of patients to find irregularities and help radiologists diagnose patients correctly. In real-time, computer vision algorithms allow autonomous cars to recognize barriers, pedestrians, and traffic signs, facilitating safe navigation and driving.

Integrating learned models into software settings where they can communicate with users or process data in real time is the first step in deploying AI-driven applications. Cloud computing platforms like Google Cloud Platform (GCP), Microsoft Azure, and Amazon Web Services (AWS) provide AI services and scalable infrastructure, making it easier to implement AI models. These platforms offer high availability, scalability, and security through managed services for model hosting, inference, and monitoring. For instance, GCP's AI Platform delivers managed services for training and deploying AI models at scale.

To sum up, creating AI-driven applications entails incorporating AI tools like computer vision, natural language processing, and machine learning into software systems to improve functionality, streamline processes, and provide insightful data. Building successful AI-driven apps requires several essential elements, including data preparation, machine learning model construction, deployment on scalable infrastructure, ethical considerations, and continual optimization.

Measuring and evaluating AI impact on business

Artificial intelligence (AI) impact on business must be measured and evaluated to determine ROI, optimize tactics, and guarantee alignment with organizational objectives. Artificial Intelligence (AI) technologies, which include computer vision, natural language processing, machine learning, and robotic process automation, can completely change how businesses operate in several industries. These technologies can boost efficiency and productivity while fostering creativity and improving client experiences.

The main parameter used to assess the impact of AI is operational efficiency. Processes can be streamlined, manual labor can be decreased, and resource allocation can be improved using AI-driven automation and optimization. For example, regular finance, HR, and customer support tasks can be automated by AI-powered robotic process automation (RPA), significantly increasing process efficiency and lowering operating costs.

Since AI technologies can personalize interactions, improve service delivery, and increase customer satisfaction, customer experience metrics are crucial in assessing the impact of AI. Chatbots and virtual assistants powered by AI can respond to consumer questions, offer instant assistance, and tailor recommendations according to user preferences. Metrics like retention rates, customer satisfaction ratings, and feedback analytics help determine how well AI is working to improve customer experiences and loyalty.

AI has a significant impact on both competitive advantage and innovation. AI technology helps companies find new revenue sources, streamline operations, and create novel products. The time to market for new AI-driven solutions, the number of patents or other intellectual property created, and market share gains attributable to AI-enabled capabilities are some examples of metrics for measuring the impact of innovation. Businesses like Tesla, which uses AI to power advanced driver-assistance systems (ADAS) and self-driving capabilities, are prime examples of how AI innovation can upend industries and reshape market leadership.

Financial indicators are crucial to assess the return on investment (ROI) of AI efforts. Businesses track the effects of AI installations on profitability, revenue growth, and cost reductions. ROI estimates are directly impacted by cost savings from AI-driven efficiency, such as lower operational or customer service costs. Metrics for measuring revenue growth include more sales due to tailored marketing or upsell possibilities by AI suggestions. Metrics like return on investment (ROI), net profit margins, and shareholder value generated by AI efforts can be used to evaluate overall profitability benefits.

When assessing AI's total commercial impact, ethical and societal implications are becoming increasingly crucial factors to consider. Responsible AI deployment is guided by moral frameworks that address issues like data protection, responsibility, transparency, and bias mitigation. Organizations use AI apps to gauge public opinion, ethical adherence, and trustworthiness. Healthcare practitioners assess the impact of AI by considering ethical aspects related to patient data protection and consent, in addition to clinical outcomes and improvements in patient care.

Finally, evaluating the impact of AI requires careful consideration of organizational readiness and capabilities growth. Companies assess their workforce upskilling initiatives, maturity in AI, and readiness for large-scale adoption of AI technologies. Employee training hours on AI, skill acquisition in data science and AI fields, and organizational agility in implementing AI breakthroughs are examples of metrics for capability development. These indicators show how well the company constantly uses AI to improve business operations and competitiveness.

In conclusion, assessing the effects of AI on business necessitates a comprehensive strategy that considers strategic alignment, qualitative advantages, quantitative measurements, and ethical issues. Companies can evaluate the worth and efficacy of AI investments by evaluating advances in operational efficiency, decision-making process enhancements, improved customer experiences, innovation outcomes, financial ROI, ethical adherence, and organizational readiness. Robust evaluation frameworks will be crucial for optimizing AI's revolutionary potential and promoting sustainable prosperity in the digital era as AI technologies advance and penetrate industries.

CHAPTER X

Future Trends and Challenges in AI

Emerging trends in AI: Quantum computing, edge AI, explainable AI

The future of technology is being shaped by new developments in artificial intelligence (AI), which open up new possibilities and capabilities in various fields. Three key developments—quantum computing, edge AI, and explainable AI—have the potential to fundamentally alter how AI systems function, interact and develop in the years to come.

The cutting edge of AI advancement is quantum computing, which provides unmatched processing capacity to tackle challenging issues beyond traditional computers' scope. Quantum computers, in contrast to conventional binary-based computing, use quantum bits, or qubits, to process information in quantum states, allowing for exponential gains in processing capacity and speed. AI applications could benefit significantly from this quantum edge, especially in machine learning, cryptography, and optimization. Algorithms for quantum machine learning can expedite processes like complex system simulation, neural network optimization, and pattern recognition.

Another revolutionary advancement in AI is edge AI, which focuses on implementing AI algorithms directly on edge devices like smartphones, Internet of Things sensors, and driverless cars. By bringing processing and data storage closer to the data source, edge computing improves privacy, lowers latency, and permits in-the-moment decision-making. When real-time data processing is necessary, like in autonomous driving for identifying and responding to road conditions or in medical equipment for in-the-moment patient monitoring and diagnosis, edge artificial intelligence (AI) is very useful.

By addressing the need for transparency and interpretability in AI systems, explainable AI (XAI) ensures that human decision-makers can comprehend and rationalize the choices made by AI algorithms. Gaining user trust, maintaining fairness, and adhering to regulatory standards depend on AI systems' capacity to explain how they arrive at their findings, which becomes increasingly complex as they are integrated into critical decision-making processes. By offering insights into AI models' internal workings, identifying variables that affect decisions, and illustrating the logic underlying predictions, XAI techniques seek to improve the interpretability of AI models.

These three new developments in AI—quantum computing, edge computing, and explainable AI—showcase AI technologies' swift development and breadth and their transformational potential, which goes beyond conventional computer paradigms. By overcoming the constraints of classical computing, quantum computing promises to transform artificial intelligence and pave the way for advances in machine learning and optimization. By enabling AI applications to function closer to data sources, edge AI improves responsiveness and permits in-the-moment decision-making in various settings. Explainable AI ensures that judgments made by AI are comprehensible and trustworthy for both users and regulators by addressing the critical need for transparency and interpretability in AI systems. These themes can spur innovation, transform industries, and open up new avenues for AI-driven solutions in the digital age as they evolve and converge with advances in AI research and development.

Challenges in AI development: Bias, fairness, transparency

Several difficulties related to AI development must be addressed to ensure the ethical, efficient, and reliable deployment of AI systems. Bias, fairness, and transparency are three significant issues in AI development that affect the dependability, equity, and accountability of AI applications in various fields.

"bias in AI" describes systemic mistakes or flaws in AI algorithms that provide unjust results; these faults frequently represent social biases in training data or design decisions. Large datasets are the source of information for AI systems, and if these datasets are skewed or unrepresentative, the AI models may reinforce and magnify preexisting biases in decision-making. In surveillance or law enforcement applications, for instance, facial recognition algorithms trained on datasets primarily including Caucasian faces may show more excellent error rates for people with darker skin tones, resulting in discriminatory consequences. To ensure that AI systems make just judgments for all demographic groups, addressing bias in AI calls for meticulous data curation, various representations in training datasets, and algorithmic tools like bias detection and mitigation.

To ensure that decisions made by AI systems do not discriminate against people or groups based on protected characteristics like race, gender, or socioeconomic position, fairness in AI refers to the equitable treatment and outcomes produced by AI systems. Establishing suitable fairness measures, evaluating algorithmic effects on various subpopulations, and implementing fairness-aware machine learning strategies are all necessary to achieve fairness in AI. For example, ensuring that the selection criteria and decision-making procedures do not unjustly harm particular demographic groups in hiring processes where AI algorithms are employed to screen job applications is critical. Algorithms with a fairness-aware design can reduce uneven effects and advance equal chances for all people, bringing AI applications into compliance with moral standards and legal requirements.

In artificial intelligence, transparency is the capacity to comprehend and analyze AI systems' decision-making process to guarantee that their actions are explicable and answerable to stakeholders. Transparency is becoming crucial for fostering acceptance and confidence among users, regulators, and the general public as AI technologies grow more sophisticated and are incorporated into essential industries like healthcare, banking, and legal systems. Explainable AI (XAI) strategies aim to improve the interpretability of AI systems by revealing how they make decisions, emphasizing significant variables, and illustrating the logic behind their predictions. Transparent AI systems promote accountability and facilitate cooperation between AI systems and human experts by enabling stakeholders to check outputs, discover biases, and highlight potential errors or limitations.

A multimodal strategy combining technological advancement, moral principles, and legal structures is needed to tackle these obstacles. Fairness, accountability, and transparency (FAT) frameworks are examples of ethical concerns that offer concepts and recommendations for developing, implementing, and ethically assessing AI systems. Regulatory authorities and industry standards are also establishing guidelines for AI governance, guaranteeing adherence to ethical and legal norms. For instance, the European General Data Protection Regulation (GDPR) requires responsibility and transparency in automated decision-making processes and the right to an explanation for those impacted by judgments made using artificial intelligence.

Furthermore, tackling prejudice, fairness, and transparency in AI development requires cooperation amongst interdisciplinary teams comprising data scientists, ethicists, policymakers, and domain specialists. Data governance techniques—such as data anonymization, variety in training datasets, and ongoing monitoring for bias detection—are essential to minimize biases and advance fairness in AI applications. To improve accountability and transparency in AI systems, algorithmic fairness and AI ethics research are developing methods for explainable AI, bias detection, and fairness-aware machine learning.

In conclusion, tackling issues like justice, bias, and transparency is critical to promoting moral AI research and guaranteeing the responsible application of AI. Stakeholders may increase trust, reduce risks, and optimize the positive effects of AI advances on society by reducing biases in training data, fostering justice in decision-making procedures, and improving transparency through explainable AI methodologies. Ethical issues and legal frameworks will be vital in determining the direction of AI research and development and creating a reliable AI ecosystem that serves people, businesses, and society at large as AI continues to advance and penetrate various industries.

Regulatory and legal aspects of AI

Artificial intelligence (AI) is causing a rapid evolution in the regulatory and legal landscape as governments and corporations struggle with AI technology's ethical, sociological, and economic ramifications. Laws and regulations are being created to guarantee that the creation and application of AI systems respect moral principles, safeguard consumer rights, and reduce any possible hazards.

Data security and privacy are two of the main issues with AI regulation. For AI systems to train algorithms and make choices, a significant amount of data—often sensitive and personal—is required. Organizations must adhere to stringent guidelines on collecting, storing, processing, and using personal data. These regulations include the California Consumer Privacy Act (CCPA) in the United States and the General Data Protection Regulation (GDPR) in Europe. These laws protect people's right to privacy, guarantee openness in data processing procedures, and give people control over their data.

Regulations intended to advance fairness, accountability, and transparency (FAT) in AI systems are driven by ethical issues in AI development. Principles for developing AI systems that respect human rights, abstain from bias and discrimination and guarantee transparency in decision-making processes are outlined in ethical guidelines, such as the EU Ethics Guidelines for Trustworthy AI and the OECD AI Principles. Regulatory organizations progressively incorporate ethical concepts into AI governance frameworks to promote responsible AI development and application across industries.

Another focus of AI legislation is safety and security, especially in areas like financial services, healthcare diagnostics, and autonomous cars. Standards and regulations are designed to guarantee that AI systems function correctly, reduce the possibility of user injury, and adhere to industry-specific safety criteria. For instance, recommended practices for risk management, cybersecurity, and system validation in AI applications are outlined in standards for the safety, dependability, and resilience of AI systems developed by the International Organization for Standardization (ISO).

In addition, frameworks for accountability and liability are developing to handle the legal ramifications of AI-driven choices and actions. When AI systems inflict pain or damage, liability questions surface, posing a duty of care among developers, users, and other parties impacted by the results of AI. Legal frameworks are developing to specify liability regimes and assign blame according to elements including carelessness, the degree of human control in AI activities, and the predictability of harm. Regulatory bodies set criteria for auditing, testing, and certifying AI technologies to guarantee adherence to safety and performance requirements. Similarly, product liability laws may impose liability on manufacturers for flaws or malfunctions in AI systems.

International cooperation and harmonization efforts are essential to address global concerns and guarantee uniformity in AI policy across jurisdictions. Organizations like the G20, OECD, and UN are encouraging national discussions and cooperation to develop shared values and policies for AI governance. These initiatives seek to advance interoperability, ease international data transfers, and tackle the worldwide moral and legal issues surrounding AI technologies.

Finally, it should be noted that AI's legal and regulatory aspects are crucial for encouraging innovation while defending moral standards, protecting consumer rights, and reducing the risks connected with AI implementation. Regulatory frameworks will guide responsible AI development and guarantee that AI systems function morally, openly, and securely as AI technologies evolve and penetrate various industries. A regulatory environment that fosters trust, creativity, and the advantages of AI developments for society can be established by policymakers and stakeholders by integrating ethical AI design, safety standards, liability frameworks, and international cooperation.

The future of AI and its potential impact on society

Artificial intelligence (AI) has enormous promise and the ability to significantly impact society in many ways, from changing economies and sectors to altering how people interact with technology and one another. As AI technologies continue to expand and mature, their data processing, decision-making, and automation capabilities are projected to bring substantial breakthroughs and efficiencies in areas such as healthcare, transportation, finance, and beyond.

The healthcare industry is one where artificial intelligence has the most significant potential social effects. AI-powered advancements in medication development, tailored treatment planning, and medical diagnostics can ultimately transform patient care. AI-powered diagnostic technologies can evaluate genomic information, patient records, and medical imaging faster and more accurately than human experts, leading to early illness detection and individualized treatment plans.

AI has the potential to revolutionize mobility in the transportation sector by accelerating the development of driverless cars and intelligent transit systems. Autonomous vehicles have the potential to improve road safety, alleviate traffic jams, and offer mobility assistance to the elderly and crippled. Transportation networks may become more effective and sustainable using AI algorithms to improve supply chain management, forecast demand trends, and optimize traffic flow.

There is a lot of discussion and worry about how AI will affect jobs and the workforce. While regular and repetitive jobs may be replaced by AI automation, which could disrupt some job sectors, it also opens up new roles and skill sets in data science, AI development, and human-AI collaboration. Initiatives aimed at reskilling and upskilling workers will ensure they have the competencies required to prosper in an AI-driven economy.

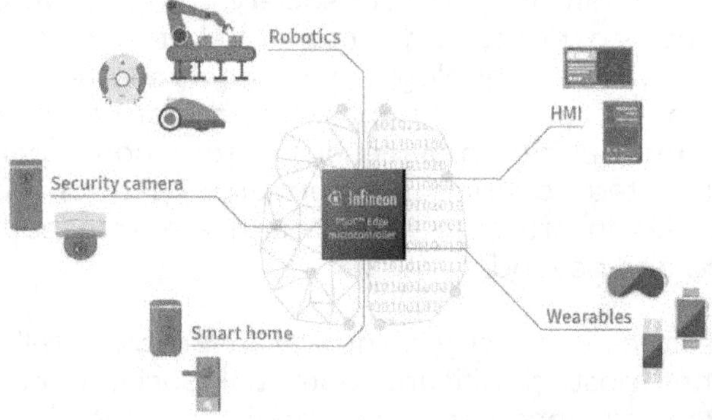

Ethical considerations surrounding AI development and deployment are essential as AI technologies become more interwoven into daily life. Regulation and careful thought must be given to issues like bias in AI algorithms, openness in decision-making procedures, and the appropriate application of AI in areas where decisions are crucial, like banking and law enforcement. Ethical frameworks and guidelines ensure that AI systems act reasonably, transparently, and in alignment with societal values and human rights.

The potential change in education and lifelong learning can also be attributed to AI. Adaptive learning platforms with AI capabilities can customize lessons, accommodate different learning preferences, and give teachers and students immediate feedback. With the help of AI algorithms, teachers can adjust their teaching tactics and interventions based on analyzing learning patterns and predicting student success.

In summary, artificial intelligence (AI) has enormous potential to advance productivity, spur innovation, and raise everyone's standard of living. While advances in AI present chances for increased productivity, cost savings, and game-changing solutions in healthcare, transportation, education, and other fields, they also present ethical, legal, and worker displacement concerns. These issues can be resolved through cooperative efforts among researchers, industry leaders, and policymakers, enabling society to fully utilize AI technology while guaranteeing their responsible, ethical, and inclusive deployment. The future of AI promises to be a transformative journey that reshapes industries, redefines human capacities, and fosters a more connected and intelligent society in the decades to come.

CONCLUSION

As we come to the end of our journey with "AI Development for the Modern World: Shaping the Future with Intelligent Systems: A Comprehensive Guide to Building and Integrating AI Solutions," we can see that the path of developing AI solutions is both rewarding and challenging. From fundamental ideas to cutting-edge technologies, and from theoretical conceptions to real-world applications, we have explored the breadth and depth of artificial intelligence together.

You now have a thorough understanding of all the key elements of artificial intelligence (AI), such as computer vision, natural language processing, machine learning, and deep learning, thanks to this book. You now know how to gather and prepare data, create and improve models, and use AI solutions successfully. You have also learned about the upcoming trends and ethical issues that will influence AI's course in the future.

You may create and use AI in various sectors using the knowledge and abilities you gain from this tutorial, leading to notable breakthroughs and efficiencies. As AI continues to evolve, so too will the opportunities and challenges it presents. Embracing the constant learning and experimenting required by this ever-changing sector will not only keep you prepared, but also make you adaptable.

By contributing to the creation of a future where intelligent systems improve and change the world, you'll be part of a dynamic and exciting field. We appreciate you starting your journey, and we wish you success in the ever-evolving world of artificial intelligence.

Thank you for buying and reading/ listening to our book. If you found this book useful/ helpful please take a few minutes and leave a review on the platform where you purchased our book. Your feedback matters greatly to us.

9 798330 265046